BLOOD BENEATH BEN NEVIS

Mark Bridgeman

Blood Beneath Ben Nevis – Mark Bridgeman & Elaine Dunsmore
© 2024. All rights reserved. The right of Mark Bridgeman to be identified as the author of the Work has been asserted in accordance with the Copyright, Designs & Patents Act 1988.

This second edition published and copyright 2024 by Tippermuir Books Ltd, Perth, Scotland.

mail@tippermuirbooks.co.uk – www.tippermuirbooks.co.uk.

No part of this publication may be reproduced or used in any form or by any means without written permission from the Publisher except for review purposes. All rights whatsoever in this book are reserved.

ISBN 978-1-913836-36-8 (paperback).

A CIP catalogue record for this book is available from the British Library.

Illustrations by Elaine Dunsmore.

Co-founders and publishers of Tippermuir Books:
Rob Hands, Matthew Mackie and Paul S Philippou.

Text design, layout, and artwork by EMB Graphics, Aberfeldy.
This edition additions by Bernard Chandler...

Printed and bound by Ashford Colour Ltd.

BLOOD BENEATH BEN NEVIS

TALES OF MURDER, MYTH AND MYSTERY
FROM LOCHABER'S DARK PAST

Mark Bridgeman

Illustrated by Elaine Dunsmore

CONTENTS

Introduction	7
Guilty or to Blame	11
The Well of the Seven Heads	17
The Unlikely Witness	24
The Silent Highwayman	34
The Nevis Construction Company	42
Morag & Lizzie	49
Massacre in a Cave	66
Ghosts in the High Street	75
The Last Outlaw	82
The Fort William Hen	89
Kinlochleven – Escape and Espionage	95
The Fort William Fires	104
The Appin Murder	109
Smugglers and Gaugers	117
The Grey Dog of Meoble	131
Monessie Camp	138
Mallaig Mysteries	146
The Inverlair Crash	157
The Expert Swordsman	164
Saved from the Plague	170
Lost Gold	175

INTRODUCTION

In the eyes of central government, Scottish and British, the Lochaber district was regarded as the epicentre of Highland disorder and disloyalty. Lochaber was full of bandits, Lochaber was very supportive of the Jacobites; therefore, Jacobites are bandits and bandits are Jacobites.

So said Professor Allan Macinnes of the Royal Society of Edinburgh in a lecture in 2013.

With a sense of history, and more than a little whiff of rebellion, I set off to explore this beautiful, remote and richly layered part of Scotland to bring together some of the most interesting stories from Lochaber's dark – and remarkable – past.

As you plunge into the pages of *Blood Beneath Ben Nevis* you will be exploring some very surprising and sometimes dark mysteries, myths and murders from the 'rough bounds' in the north, to the furthest point west on the British mainland. From the bottom of the deepest loch in Scotland, Loch Morar, to the top of the highest mountain, Ben Nevis. From the bustling streets of Lochaber's capital, and largest town, Fort William, to its remote villages, hamlets and crofts.

There are surprising revelations, interesting characters and places, and some common themes that seem to permeate many of the stories. *Uisge Beatha* (whisky) is one thread that runs through many. Sometimes as a form of income, sometimes as a catalyst to much darker deeds and sometimes merely as an excuse.

The harsh measures of the British Government and the redcoat soldiers to douse any remaining spark of rebellion after the '45 rebellion, was felt more harshly in Lochaber than almost anywhere else in Scotland. The area symbolised the struggle more than any other and is still marked with the memories, and scars from the days following Bonnie Prince Charlie's raising of the Jacobite standard at Glenfinnan on 19th August 1745. There is a flavour of the rebellion, the aftermath, and the resentment that colours several of the stories in this book. The suppression of the Highlander's way of life took many forms, from the banning of tartan plaids and bagpipes (the 1747 Act of Proscription, sometimes called the Dis-clothing Act), to the Disarming Act and the repression of the Gaelic language.

I found while writing the book, that a person would occasionally appear in more than one story. In one case, a character makes the leap (literally!) from the pages of this book into the geographical territory of my previous book, *The River Runs Red*.

After a feast of tales involving murder, treachery, legend (often with a strong basis in fact), strange coincidence, fire, disease, clan warfare, smuggling, and, of course, rebellion, the book concludes with a treasure hunt in which all of the known clues in the search for the legendary Jacobite lost gold are collected together in one place.

Many have tried to locate the lost gold, worth many millions of pounds. Perhaps someone who reads this book will be the fortunate one who recovers the missing treasure, finding fame and fortune.

Mark Bridgeman

GUILTY OR TO BLAME

On the evening of Tuesday 27th January 1846, Alexander Campbell, his father John and Alexander MacMaster, met John Macdonald and his son Angus (who was a shepherd) for drinks at the *Bridge of Nevis Inn* in Fort William. The other men were all crofters or labourers and it had been another busy day of toil. The weather had been unusually mild that month, and they had been able to accomplish more than was usual for the time of year. Once at the inn they drank several whiskies and their behaviour became gradually more boisterous. Young Angus Macdonald waved his shepherd's stick over his head, in an animated fashion, accidently striking one of the group. He was told, in no uncertain terms, to put the stick down as tempers started to fray. Conscious that they needed a change of scenery, the men left the Inn, out into the cold night air, and decided to walk to the Lochy Ferry Inn, opposite the Lochkeeper's cottage. It was closer to the men's homes at Lochyside in Kilmalie.

By the time the men had reached the Lochy Ferry Inn the effects of the alcohol had markedly increased. Now rowdy and loud they pushed open the door and entered the small inn. Through the entrance the men made their way into the 'middle-room', a small room measuring just 11 feet by 10, with a closet and a further entrance to another room (known as the 'inner-room'). The candlelit room was furnished with a table, two chests and several chairs. The group removed the chairs, pushing them into the closet. With that they ordered drinks from the barmaid Jane Cameron. There seemed to be a disagreement between John Campbell and John MacDonald over payment for the whisky, and Jane Cameron retired to the kitchen at the back of the building, without having been paid. Mrs Cameron, the wife of the owner, and her 11-year-old son Donald were also in the kitchen. She heard raised voices and decided to fetch her husband Ewen who was at the Lochkeeper's cottage opposite.

When the owner Ewen Cameron arrived, John Campbell was still refusing to pay for the drinks, swearing and cursing and shouting that 'the whisky was no good'. His son, Alexander Campbell, then removed his pea-jacket and was heard to say in Gaelic 'if it is fighting they want, they shall get enough of it'. A fight then erupted between the men. MacMaster and Angus MacDonald grappled in one corner of the room. Punches were thrown and the two men, locked in a wrestle, knocked over the table. The candles were thrown from the table, extinguishing as they hit the stone floor, plunging the room into near darkness. John MacDonald punched John Campbell, knocking him to the floor, and immediately jumped on top of him. The barmaid hurried to get help and to fetch more candles to light the room. As she did so, she cried out 'Murder! Murder!' several times. Ewen Cameron, on entering the room saw John MacDonald knelt on top of John Campbell, his knees pressed hard against the other man's chest, his left hand holding him by the shoulder, his right hand raining down punches to the face. Ewen Cameron rushed between them, pulling MacDonald off. By this time John Campbell was unconscious. There was vivid red blood on the side of his face, a bleeding wound on his left temple and a considerable amount of blood on the floor. He shouted for his wife to fetch the doctor and the police at once.

The other men continued to struggle for several minutes, until they too realised the gravity of the situation. Cameron, the innkeeper, deliberately stood close to the motionless body of John Campbell. He did not want the men to further injure, or move, the unconscious man. This action would prove to be a crucial and important point at the later trial.

Dr Kennedy from Fort William arrived and immediately began to tend to the patient. The doctor asked John MacDonald what had occurred, and he replied: "If I have done it, I have no recollection of it".

Campbell was in severe difficulties and was removed to

a bedroom above the inn. He died at five o'clock the following morning. John MacKay, the superintendent of police from Fort William, arrested John MacDonald, taking him first to the cells in town and then to Inverness Jail. Speaking in Gaelic, MacDonald explained to the officer: "I am guilty; although I did not strike the man with the stick, I did so with my hands and feet." The police officer warned MacDonald not to speak until he had been properly cautioned, but MacDonald simply repeated his remarks, claiming: "I would make the same statement again, even if otherwise advised."

MacDonald was charged with murder and the case came before Lord MacKenzie at the Inverness Circuit Court. A sizeable crowd gathered to witness the events. Murder trials always drew large crowds, everyone anxious to see the murderer face-to-face. The charge of murder was read out and John MacDonald (who only spoke Gaelic and had to be translated throughout the proceedings) answered, "I am guilty, or to blame". Many present were unable to decide if he meant 'guilty' to the charge of murder, or merely meant to accept the blame for accidentally causing John Campbell's death. The point was not clarified, but probably prejudiced his case.

Defendants, at this point (and until 1883), were considered as being from the 'low classes' and therefore were not allowed to speak in their own defence, as it was felt they would undoubtedly prejudice their own case. Clearly, MacDonald did so here, although the recently introduced (1836) right for a defence lawyer to sum up and address the jury at least offered some redress in this case.

Dr Kennedy was called to the stand on three occasions, in three separate roles (an unusual circumstance in a murder trial). Firstly, as a witness to explain his version of events, secondly, as a character witness for the accused (who he told the court was hard working and of previous good character), and thirdly, as a medical expert. Dr Kennedy read a portion of the post-mortem report to the court:

Death had been caused through laceration of the liver, produced by the fracture of the seventh and eighth ribs, and consequent flow of blood into the abdomen. Weighty pressure, such as a man sitting upon the ribs, would have produced the injuries spoken of in this report and having been sustained by the deceased in that region.

The defence argued that the injuries to the victim's chest could have been caused by the tread of another man accidentally standing upon him during the struggle, and that there was no proof that MacDonald was actually to blame for the injury that caused John Campbell's death. However, the earlier and crucial testimony of the innkeeper (who had stood by the victim's side) proved fatal for the defendant.

Whether John MacDonald had grabbed his son's shepherd's stick and hit John Campbell with it, could not be proved by court. The witnesses were not sure. MacDonald denied doing so, however it was argued that a blow from the stick might account for the gash to the side of the victim's head.

Following the summation by Lord MacKenzie, he instructed the jury to retire and consider their verdict. After a short recess they returned a verdict of guilty, not of murder, but of culpable homicide. (Scottish juries often preferred to recommend this lesser penalty. In Scottish murder trials, the death penalty was only used in approximately a quarter of all cases.)

John MacDonald was sentenced to 18 months' imprisonment. The drunken nature of all the men being taken into account. Perhaps a lighter sentence than might be expected for a similar offence today.

THE WELL OF THE SEVEN HEADS

By the side of the A82, on the north shore of Loch Oich, a mile or so from Invergarry, sits a strange monument called Tobar nan Ceann (The Well of the Seven Heads). The well was erected by Colonel Alasdair MacDonell of Glengarry in 1812, in memory of his ancestors. The B-listed monument comprises an obelisk of polished ashlar, topped by seven carved stone heads together with a hand clutching a dagger. Set on a square base, the monument bears an inscription in Latin, English, French and Gaelic explaining the full horror of the Keppoch murders.

Donald Glas, the eleventh chief of the MacDonells of Keppoch (a branch of the clan MacDonald), was a well respected Highland chief. In 1661, as was the custom among Highland hierarchy, he sent his sons Alexander and Ranald to be educated in France. However, Donald Glas passed away in 1663 and his sons were recalled to Scotland. As the boys were not considered old enough to oversee the affairs of the clan, that duty passed to Alisdair Buidhe, their uncle, although the Privy Council had recognised Alexander as rightful chief of the Keppoch lands. Unfortunately, this arrangement was not to the liking of a branch of the clan known as the Sioll Dughaill family, who themselves coveted secret ambitions for chieftaincy of the clan. They were also encouraged in their ambition by other discontented clan members.

When the elder brother Alexander reached the age of accession to the leadership of the clan, he threw a banquet to celebrate. Among the many guests were the father of the Sioll Dughaill family and his six sons. During the feast, by a devious prior arrangement, the Sioll Dughaill picked a quarrel with Alexander and Ranald, mocking the French manners and customs they had adopted. During the fight, Alexander and his brother were stabbed. Alexander 33 times and Ranald 28 times. A royal commission report, issued by the Privy Council on 29 July 1665 described the events as follows:

Upon the 25th day of September, 1663 years, to the place of Keppoch, armed with swords, dirks and other weapons invasive, and there cruelly and unmercifully and by way of hamsuken*, within the said place of Keppoch, invading and assaulting and setting upon Alexander MacDonald of Keppoch and Ranald MacDonald, his brother, by giving the said Alexander 33 great wounds and to the said Ranald MacDonald, his brother, 28 wounds, of which they immediately dyed upon the place.

(*hamsuken – an old Sottish legal term for assaulting a person in their own house)

The Sioll Dughaill announced that the boys' deaths had been an unfortunate accident. Alasdair Buidhe, their uncle, was also suspected of being involved, but no proof could be found and no charge was ever brought against him.

For some time, and unusually, it appeared that the death of the two boys would go largely ignored and unavenged. Many members of the Keppoch MacDonald clan felt that the boys were softened by their time in France and simply did not possess the warlike leadership qualities of a clan chief.

There was one man, however, who was certain that young Alexander and Ranald had been murdered. The Keppoch bard, poet and storyteller Iain Lom (also known as Bald Iain) wanted revenge on behalf of the boys. He sought support locally from the MacDonell chief Glengarry, but Glengarry would not move against the Sioll Dughaill family, as he could not be certain the deaths were deliberate and not accidents. Undeterred, Iain Lom visited Sir James MacDonald of Sleat, at Duntulm Castle on the Isle of Skye, and appealed to the chief's emotions in dramatic and biblical language:

Abel is cold and his blood is crying in vain for vengeance. Cain is hot and red-handed and hundreds are lukewarm as the black goat's milk.

After several attempts at persuasion, Sir James agreed to approach the Privy Council in Edinburgh for permission to seek retribution under the law. A 'State Commission of Fire and Sword' was granted so that Iain Lom and Sir James could seek 'ample and summary revenge'.

So, in July 1665 the two men with 50 of MacDonald's troops, all suitably armed, set out for the home of the Sioll Dughaill family at Inverlair Lodge. The small army smashed down the substantial barricades around the house and slew the murderers of Alexander and Ranald – in their own house. Iain Lom cut off the heads of the father and his six sons and had their bodies buried in a small knoll close to Inverlair Lodge. This alone was not enough for Iain Lom, he wanted to display his gruesome trophies to MacDonell of Glengarry (who had refused to help him two years earlier). He fashioned a rope of heather, then tied the hair of the victims dismembered heads to it, before setting off to meet Glengarry. Just before arriving, he decided to wash the blood off the seven heads and stopped at a small well, close to the shore of Loch Oich. In Pagan times, Celts believed that the head was the home of a person's spirit, so that possession of an enemy's head ensured power over him, as well as being a hugely symbolic gesture.

From that moment on, the well became known as 'The Well of the

Seven Heads' and was eventually marked by the monument built by Colonel MacDonell in 1812. A tunnel to channel the water was also constructed under the well and can be accessed by visitors. Iain Lom, after showing the severed heads to Glengarry, had them sent to the Isle of Skye to show Sir James MacDonald that justice had been served. From there, the heads were sent to Edinburgh, where they were displayed on the gallows on the site where the Playhouse Theatre now stands. The clerk of the Privy Council noted, on 7th December 1665 that "the heads of the said persons be affixt on the gallows standing on the gallowlie betwixt Leith and Edinburgh."

The story did not end there, however.

It is a little known fact that, despite exacting such bloodthirsty revenge, Iain Lom's sister was actually married to the father of the Sioll Dughaill family! Lom would later compose a mournful Gaelic lament in memory of the two boys, entitled *Mort na Ceapaich* (The Death of Keppoch). He died in 1709 and was buried in the graveyard of Cille Choirill (the church of St Cyril), close to Roy Bridge.

During the nineteenth century a mound of earth, close to Inverlair Lodge, between Inverness and Fort William, was excavated by Dr Smith from Fort William. The digging revealed the headless skeletons of seven victims. This added much credence to the tale and led to a renewed interest in the story and especially to the Well of the Seven Heads. Stories that the well was haunted were given further weight by the death of two motor cyclists in a collision, in close proximity to the monument, in 1928. Conditions were fine and no one could understand how the two cyclists could possibly have collided on such a straight road, unless they had been momentarily distracted.

In 1930 the position of the well was moved slightly, to allow for construction of the new Glasgow to Inverness road. Several workmen refused to work on the site, after claiming they has seen headless apparitions close to the well. In 1980 there was a further death on the same stretch of road, when a car and lorry collided, in perfect conditions, with no obvious reason for the crash.

In an unusual aside to the story, Inverlair Lodge – scene of the massacre of the Sioll Dughaill family - received another unwelcome visitor in May 1941. After an incredible and secretive flight from Germany, Rudolf Hess, the deputy leader of Nazi Germany (second only to Adolf Hitler) was interned there for a time. He was placed under the guard of the Commandos, who were stationed there during the Second World War.

The monument at the Well of the Seven Heads bears the following inscription:

As a memorial of the ample and summary vengeance which, in the swift course of feudal justice, inflicted by the order of Lord McDonell and Aross, overtook the perpetrators of a foul murder of the Keppoch Family, a branch of the powerful and illustrious clan of which his lordship was the chief. This monument is erected by Colonel McDonell of Glengarry, XVII Mac-Mhic-Alaister, his successor and representative, in the Year of Our Lord 1812. The heads of the Seven Murderers were presented at the feet of the noble Chief in Glengarry Castle after having been washed in this spring; and ever since that event, which took place in the seventeenth century, it has been known by the name of Tobar-nan-Ceann or the Well of The Seven Heads.

THE UNLIKELY WITNESS

The justice dealt out by the British government to the Highlanders, following the Jacobite's defeat at the Battle of Culloden in 1746, was often harsh and uncompromising. The Disarming Act imposed on the Scottish represented nothing less than an attempt to dismantle the ancient clan structure. Highlanders were forbidden to carry weapons such as muskets, dirks, the Lochaber Axe or the famous broadsword. Highland dress was outlawed. Playing of the bagpipes was banned. Prayers for the Hanoverian monarch in London became compulsory before school lessons every day. Gaelic was outlawed. Fines, imprisonment, and exile awaited those clansmen who dared defy the new laws. Even worse was the justice dispensed to any Scot found guilty of the murder of an English Redcoat soldier.

Except that is, for two fortunate Highlanders who escaped British justice, thanks to the evidence given at their trial by a Lochaber man named Alexander MacPherson.

Among the regiments tasked with stamping out the last sparks of the Jacobite rebellion in the years following Culloden, was the 1st Regiment of Foot under Lieutenant-General John Guise. A unit of the regiment, led by Sergeant Arthur Davis, patrolled a vast and remote area between Loch Laggan and Inverey, to the east. On the morning of 28th September 1749, Sergeant Davis set out, along with his unit, to rendezvous with a detachment of English soldiers at Glenshee. However, when the men arrived, Sergeant Davis was no longer with them. The remaining men in his unit could only say that Davis had left them, in order to pursue his favourite sport of solitary hunting. They reported hearing a gunshot. They waited for a while, but when the Sergeant did not return, they scoured the district but could find no trace of him. Eventually they were forced to continue their journey and report their findings.

Sergeant Davis was a well-liked man among both the rank and file and the officers above him. He was a 'gentleman' by birth, well educated, courageous and a lover of sport. Davis was a 'dandy' dresser, known for his hat, bordered with fine, white trim and silver button (engraved with his initials ARD), blue surtout coat, striped waistcoat, silver pocket watch, hair tied back in a black silk ribbon, and two gold rings. He was in the habit of carrying his gold coins with him, at all times, in a leather purse – which he made no attempt to hide. In a separate green silk purse he carried silver coins, which he used for his day-to-day expenses. Sergeant Davis was not unpopular with the Highlanders he encountered, in fact, he was well liked and held a great affection for Scotland. On the day in question, he was dressed in all his finery, with a vest of roe skin, highland brogues with silver buckles, finished off with silver buttons on his tunic.

A command order was issued and a search was carried out for the missing Sergeant. However, after four days the patrols were unable to find any trace of him and the search was abandoned. Rumours spread that he may have deserted, however his wife knew this was unlikely:

He could never be under any temptation to desert as he was much esteemed and beloved by all his officers, and had good reason to believe he would have promoted to the rank of sergeant-major upon the first vacancy.

It was also conjectured that he may have been murdered by two local Highlanders called Duncan Terig (alias Clerk) and Alexander Bane MacDonald. The men's behaviour, before and after the murder, had aroused suspicion. Duncan Clerk, prior to the disappearance of Sergeant Davis, had been heavily in debt. As was later testified in court:

He was not possessed of any visible funds or effects which could enable him to stock a farm before the period of the said murder, yet soon thereafter he took and obtained a lease from Lord Bracco, of a farm called the Craggan, for which he was bound to pay thirty pounds Scots of yearly rent; as also thereafter he obtained a lease of the farm of Gleney, from Farquharson of Inverey, for which at present he was bound to pay a yearly rent, or tack duty, of one hundred and five merks Scots. (approximately £2,000 today)

(A merk was a Scottish silver coin, worth 13 shillings)

Duncan Clerk's wife Elizabeth had been given a gold ring by her husband which had been seen by several witnesses. The ring had an unusual raised heart design on the bezel, exactly matching the ring worn by Sergeant Davis. During the later trial Elspeth Macara, a maid to Duncan Clerk, saw the ring being worn by Elizabeth Clerk. Elspeth was surprised, thinking that Elizabeth Clerk had only a brass ring. Elizabeth Clerk explained that the ring had belonged to her mother.

Alexander Bane MacDonald, two years after the disappearance of Sergeant Davis, was observed, while drinking in an inn, holding a penknife which matched the description of a penknife belonging to the Sergeant. It had been fashioned with a stamp for a letter seal at the butt of the handle, making it highly distinctive. MacDonald, in court, denied that he had ever owned such an item – claiming that he could not read or write, therefore had no need for a seal.

In 1751 Alexander MacPherson entered the employment of Duncan Clerk. During a heated conversation MacPherson claimed he was offered £20 as an inducement to *'hold his tongue of what he knew of Sergeant Davis.'* MacPherson also claimed that he witnessed Clerk holding a leather purse containing English guineas and gold coins.

Rumours and circumstantial evidence were mounting. MacDonald had been seen in possession of a fowling piece, thought to belong to Sergeant Davis (a shotgun used for hunting wildfowl). Both men had a reputation locally as thieves and bandits. Yet, without a body, the evidence could all be explained away. The men could easily claim to have found the items discarded on the ground. Indeed, a woman called Isobel Ego found Sergeant's Davis's white hat on Christie's Hill, near to Inverey, but clearly she had nothing to do with his disappearance.

The hat, however, would prove to be the catalyst in a chain of events that would lead Duncan Clerk and Alexander Bane MacDonald to the High Court in Edinburgh. Isobel Ego showed the white hat to Duncan Clerk, who took it from her and hid it under a large stone close to a nearby burn. A short while afterwards, some children playing discovered the hat and showed it to Mr James Small, the factor for the Strowan Estate, and a good friend of Sergeant Davis. James Small had been a close acquaintance of

Sergeant Davis and knew immediately that the hat being found in such close proximity to the home of Duncan Clerk was highly suspicious. He began a quest for justice on behalf of his missing friend.

In the summer of the following year Alexander MacPherson found some human remains on Christie's Hill, near Inverey. He knew that Sergeant Davis had been murdered in that vicinity the previous year, and immediately suspected the bones belonged to the missing soldier. There was little flesh left on the body, thanks to the effect of decomposition and scavenging animals. The bones had been scattered, however there was still mouse coloured hair on the skull, tied in a ribbon, parts of a uniform, brogues and other tell-tale signs. Alexander MacPherson consulted his closest friends. Should they tell the authorities? John Growar and Donald Farquharson both agreed that they should have nothing to do with the matter, for fear of reprisals. They, or their families could be blamed by the British government. The men decided to keep their gruesome discovery a secret. They attempted to move the remains to a damp, peaty part of the hillside – in the hope that the skeleton would become overgrown – however the remains broke apart as they tried to lift them. Sergeant Davis was left to rest on the hill.

However, Alexander MacPherson became increasingly restless about the guilty secret he had carried during the days and weeks following his discovery of the body. Eventually, racked with guilt, he was woken one night by the appearance of a man, dressed in blue, who appeared at his bedside. The man beckoned him to come outside. MacPherson rose and followed the figure to the doorway. As he opened the door, to a clear moonlit night, the stranger turned and said "I am Sergeant Davis" then, pointing to a tract of swampy moorland at the foot of Christie's Hill, added "You will find my bones there; go and bury them at once, for I can have no peace, nor will I give you any, until my bones are buried, and you may get Donald Farquharson to help you." With that the apparition vanished.

The following morning MacPherson recovered the remains of the Sergeant and laid them neatly on a bed of soil and moss, but made no attempt to bury them. A few nights later the apparition again appeared to MacPherson and demanded angrily: "Why have my bones not been buried?"

MacPherson this time plucked up enough courage to speak, "Who murdered you?"

The ghost replied, "Duncan Terig and Alexander MacDonald." The vision then vanished.

Isobel McHardie, who also lived in the same bothy as MacPherson, is said to have witnessed the ghost of Sergeant Davis on its second visit to MacPherson.

The very next day MacPherson told Donald Farquharson about his visitation and the men buried the body on the hillside. Superstition forbade them from burying an 'unkent' (unknown) body in a graveyard. Despite local speculation and gossip, for almost four years the pair kept silent until James Small, who had heard persistent rumours about the story, questioned the men more closely. Overcome with remorse, MacPherson admitted the whole affair. James Small, with the evidence of Sergeant Davis's ghost, was convinced he had enough evidence to commence legal proceedings against Duncan Clerk and Alexander Bane MacDonald. A trial date was set for 11th June 1754 at the Lords of Session in Edinburgh.

Perhaps using some of his ill-gotten gains, Duncan Clerk hired the services of Alexander Lockhart, Scotland's most eminent advocate, as his defence counsel. Lockhart had already defended many of those imprisoned in Carlisle following the '45 rebellion and subsequent defeat at Culloden.

The evidence provided in court by the prosecution seemed to be damning. Witness after witness identified items, found in Clerk and MacDonald's possession, as belonging to Sergeant Davis. His money purse, fowling piece, penknife and distinctive gold ring. Clerk's sudden and mysterious wealth and the men's previous bad character all seemed enough to condemn them to the gallows.

However, the evidence of Alexander MacPherson for the prosecution proved to be the turning point in the trial. MacPherson solemnly gave the testimony of the ghost of Sergeant Davis, relating the evidence provided by the apparition to him. The courtroom was stunned as MacPherson (who could only speak Gaelic and had his words translated for the benefit of the court) repeated the words told to him by the ghost; *'Duncan Terig and Alexander MacDonald'*. Alexander Lockhart rose from his seat to begin his cross-examination:

"What language did the ghost speak in?", he asked MacPherson.

MacPherson promptly replied, "As good Gaelic as ever I heard in Lochaber!"

"Pretty good for the ghost of an ENGLISH SERGEANT!" retorted Lockhart, amid roars of laughter from the courtroom.

Despite the damning evidence of the dead man's property found in the possession of the accused, Lockhart persuaded the jury that the case should be laughed out of court. The jury agreed and returned a verdict of 'not guilty'. The Right Honourable Lord William Adam was forced to dismiss the prisoners from the bar and they walked away as free men.

In a footnote to the story Lockhart later admitted that, "but for that lucky joke about the ghost, and the capital I made of it, I could never have secured an acquittal, for I had not the slightest doubt that the prisoners were guilty."

Lockhart refused to let the matter drop there, however. Two days after the trial he sent a formal letter of complaint to the court in Edinburgh, alleging that Sergeant Davis's friend James Small had bullied and intimidated witnesses, in an effort to obtain their evidence. He added that he considered Small meant to blacken his client's name and 'fix upon him for ever the basest and worst of characters.' As a result, Small suffered the embarrassment of two week's detention in Edinburgh Tolbooth and an order 'not to resent the injury done to him in any manner.'

Sir Walter Scott, the novelist, who was also a member of the bar, became fascinated in the case and produced a written account in 1831, for the benefit of fellow members of the Bannatyne Club (a society founded by Scott for the publication of rare and interesting texts).

Surprisingly, this is not the only case in which the evidence of a ghost has been called upon in court. There is one other. In 1693, in the trial of John Cole as an accessory in the murder of Dr Clenche, a witness claimed that the ghost of the dead man had told her that John Cole had taken part in his murder. In this case, however, the judge ruled the evidence inadmissible, unless the ghost himself could be brought into the courtroom to swear an oath and take the witness stand!

THE SILENT HIGHWAYMAN

During the early 19th century, cholera first reached Europe from the Indian subcontinent. Attempts were made to stem the arrival of the disease onto British shores. Incoming ships were quarantined in an effort to halt the spread. However, the busy port of London found it almost impossible to manage the huge number of vessels arriving every day. The first identified case of cholera in Britain was reported in October 1831, when ship's keelman William Sproat contracted the disease and died just three days later.

The public were warned to avoid contact with any persons coming from the Continent, including any communication with smugglers. Sufferers displayed symptoms including 'stomach cramps, looseness of the bowels, vomiting, severe pain in the limbs and severe dehydration that, if left untreated, may suddenly assume a fatal form.'

There was no known cure, and the sense of panic among both the populace and the government was palpable. Cholera was, wrongly, thought to be airborne. While the residents of London, Liverpool and Glasgow began to fear contact with travellers and neighbours alike, they continued to drink water that had been contaminated with sewage. Basement cesspits overflowed into rivers that provided drinking water for large sections of the population. In 1831, The *London Gazette* published a Board of Health report that attributed cholera to, "the poor, ill-fed, and unhealthy part of the population, and especially those who have been addicted to the drinking of spirituous liquors, and indulgence in irregular habits".

In February 1832, the Cholera Morbus Prevention Act became law and allowed some powers to local Boards of Health, but it was to have little impact on the upcoming epidemic. Surely though, even this most virulent of diseases could not reach the remote and sparsely populated region of Lochaber? Whilst news of the cholera epidemic had reached officials and those who were able to read newspapers, a vast cross-section of the population would doubtless have been entirely ignorant.

A ship entering Loch Linnhe docked at Fort William early in 1832. The vessel offloaded linen, among other provisions. It is not known if quarantine measures were in place, but it is unlikely as the ship had not sailed from Europe, but from either Glasgow or Greenock. The captain of a ship that had recently docked at Crinan Harbour had already died of the disease. Within days of the ship's arrival at Fort William the first cases of cholera were diagnosed. Without proper understanding of the disease's *modus operandi* it was assumed that the linen offloaded from the ship had brought the illness into the town. Cholera is usually waterborne and, most likely, arrived in tainted water or sewage transference.

(Perhaps the story of the disease arriving in Fort William via tainted linen is a merging of two stories, over time? - see chapter *Saved From The Plague*)

To stop the spread of the disease local officials were able to divert money from the burgh's Poor Relief Fund. Proposals were put in place. Some, it seems, were effective and some misplaced. In Morvern the Parochial Board wrote to tenants with the following advice:

to press upon the people who reside on the estate the necessity of cleansing their dwellings from all impurities and from stagnant water and ... to issue to each family such small quantity of lime as maybe requisite for whitewashing the inside of their houses.

The following circular was printed and distributed to as many houses as possible in Lochaber, and the west of Scotland, during February 1832 and graphically outlines the 19th century understanding of the spread of disease:

Preventives – Be clean in your person. Wear flannels next to the skin. Keep the bowels well defended from cold, and never sit down with wet or cold feet. Abstain from small beer, and use spiritous liquours very moderately. Use no water that is not pure. The use of strong broth and butcher meat is salutary. Avoid raw vegetables, and boil well what you eat. Do not go out in the morning without breaking your fast. Avoid getting wet, or going out at night. Avoid also large towns, infected places, and public houses.

Piggeries, Dunghills, and Cess-pools ought to be at some distance and frequently cleaned. Let the house be regularly ventilated, and well swept. When you wash it, choose a sunny day, and do it in the morning, so that there may be no damp when you shut up at night. Keep your doors dry.

Symptoms and treatment – Cholera generally begins with giddiness, languor, and uneasiness in the bowels, accompanied by looseness more or less. When such symptoms appear, no time ought to be lost in sending for medical advice – but in the meantime, 30 drops of Laudanum, and 3 teaspoonfuls of Castor Oil may be taken in a little hot brandy and water. Go to bed immediately, and keep yourself warm. Heated bricks or hot bottles may be applied, or bags of hot bran or salt. Place a mustard blister on the stomach. Let your drink consist of warm barley-water in small portions. Cold water is dangerous, and Salts must on no account be taken.

Should the Castor Oil be thrown up, take 30 drops of plain Laudanum. Families ought to provide themselves with Laudanum and the other articles, as all depends on taking the disease at the first.

Laudanum was a tincture of opium. While it could

certainly ease the most obvious symptom of cholera - diarrhoea - it really was not a cure.

Cholera did not just confine itself to just the towns, however. The crofting hamlet of Blarmacfoldach, in the Mamore Hills between Fort William and Kinlochleven, boasted a population of more than 800 people in 1830. The outbreak decimated the inhabitants and the numbers never recovered. Today, as a result of the outbreak and other factors, the population now stands at less than 30.

In October 1832 a young mother, Susan Cameron, from Fort William, tried to escape the plague by fleeing the town and heading to the Braes of Lochaber, carrying her infant son with her. She intended to stay with her mother in a tiny crofter's cottage in Killmonivaig, near the River Spean. Unfortunately, the young woman was already infected with the disease. She died shortly after arriving, as did her son. A great many more people in the community also became infected as a result of a simple misunderstanding of the need to quarantine sufferers, but miraculously the woman's mother survived. Such was the fear of the disease that no one could be found to bury the bodies. Eventually, after much pleading from the woman's mother, the parish clergyman Rev MacInytre, Dr Kennedy from Fort William, and a kindly neighbour, Captain MacDonnell, agreed to help bury the dead, but only in the grounds of the croft and not in the nearby graveyard. A basic coffin was constructed from an old carpenter's bench and the three gentlemen hastily dug a grave with their own hands. The mother and child were laid to rest, not in a shroud (as was common practice) but wrapped in the blanket in which they had both died. Sadly, the neighbour succumbed to the disease soon after. Dr Kennedy did survive, but did himself die some years later when helping others during an outbreak of typhus in Fort William.

Ten years after this sad incident the woman's mother passed away. Her son knew that she would want to be buried next to her daughter, Susan Cameron, and tiny grandson. He applied for permission to have the bodies exhumed, so the three could be buried together in the nearby churchyard. Such was the fear of cholera victims that many superstitions existed, and no one could actually recall seeing a victim's body after it had been buried. However, the sight which greeted those present at the exhumation shocked and haunted them all for many years. The bodies of both the mother and son were perfectly and completely preserved – as if they had only just been buried. Both mother and son were without a single sign of deterioration, apart from a single shocking occurrence. Both victims' skin had turned completely black. The shocking spectacle haunted those who witnessed it for many years. Some attributed it to the unusually peaty soil, some as a sign from God or the Devil.

During October 1832 the *Inverness Courier* carried a 'snapshot' of the effects of the disease, reporting figures from the Board of Health for Lochaber, Fort William and Inverness during the previous month: "Total cases from commencement 514; deaths 161; recoveries 339; still remaining ill 14". The mortality rate of 30% was actually less severe than that experienced in the larger cities.

By December of 1832 the outbreak of cholera seems to have subsided. The *Inverness Courier* reported that: "now that the cholera has departed, the young men have leisure and courage to look forward; and prepare for domestic happiness. Little else is going on but marriage and thoughts of marriage." However, there were further recurrences in 1848, 1853 and 1856. Industrial towns and fishing ports in Scotland were usually worst affected. Glasgow's thriving port, busy with cargo ships from all reaches of the British Empire, and overcrowded living conditions in the tenements were mainly responsible for the spread of cholera throughout the west coast of Scotland. The disease became known as The Silent Highwayman (mainly due to a cartoon that appeared in *Punch* magazine), as it seemed to arrive unexpectedly, attack

lonely communities, threatening and robbing from all the inhabitants without prejudice.

The understanding of the disease did improve, but only very gradually. It wasn't until the creation of better quality housing and adequate sanitation facilities in the larger cities, later in the century, that the disease was finally tamed and its spread to regions such as Lochaber was finally halted. Lochaber could think itself lucky. The 1832 epidemic killed 10,000 people in Scotland, 3,000 in Glasgow alone. Whilst 50% of those people infected died, as a result of catching the disease, the numbers in Lochaber were comparatively small, owing to the sparse population and the distances between communities. It is still believed somewhere between 500 - 800 people lost their lives in a nine-month period.

THE NEVIS
CONSTRUCTION COMPANY

Fort William acted as an unwitting accomplice in a cruel deception that the majority of people in the town were never even aware of. As the post Great War depression was beginning to bite and many men lay idle, desperate for employment, a heartless conman chose the town he thought had treated him so unfairly to be the central figure in his elaborate ruse. To tell the full story of John Slaven, however, we must start in Ireland during the Potato Famine of the 1840s.

The Slaven family were notorious in Ireland. John's father and uncle had narrowly escaped a death sentence following a robbery in Tipperary in 1842. Other brothers, uncles and cousins had been involved in assaults, robberies and frequent arrests for drunken fights and breaches of the peace. John Slaven was born in 1855 and, like so many others, travelled across the Irish Channel to Scotland, searching for work. He landed in Greenock around 1872, still aged only 17, and was almost immediately in trouble with the law. He was arrested twice in Cathcart Street for being an 'unlicensed pedlar' and on both occasions chose a seven-day prison sentence in preference to a 15-shilling fine, where he least he was fed and warm.

By the summer of 1877 he had migrated to Dundee where he once again found himself on the wrong side of the law. He had no fixed residence, sleeping rough and stealing what items he could, in order to buy food and alcohol. During 1877 he was charged on four separate occasions for robbery, the most bizarre being the theft of doormats! Slaven walked the length of Forebank Road, King Street and William Street removing doormats in order to sell them. He received a 60-day prison sentence.

During the next 10 years John Slaven appeared in court and was jailed a multitude of times, for assaults, drunken violence and robbery. Most seriously of all, he was charged in 1887 for an attempted murder while working on board a ship. Slaven stabbed the man in the stomach but was able to show in court that he had been defending himself against a violent attack.

Anxious to move away from the Glasgow area after having just been released from another 14 days incarceration, this time for an assault at Gartsherrie Station in Coatbridge, Slaven arrived in Fort William in late 1887, his steamer landing alongside the pier on Loch Linnhe. He was soon arrested for begging in the street

By 1892 there was a prospect of employment within the local area, on the construction of the West

Highland Railway. The work would be arduous and dangerous, in cold and unforgiving terrain. Slaven, it appears, did not seem interested in hard physical toil and following yet more charges of vagrancy, slipped away from Fort William during a scarlet fever outbreak in 1894.

Following the fatal stabbing of a fellow navvy, Bernard Hughes, at the Blairenbathie Mine near Dunfermline in 1897, John Slaven once again narrowly avoided a prison sentence as it could not be proven that he was the one who delivered the fatal blow and he was released without charge.

For a substantial period of time following this incident, Slaven continued to work as a navvy, helping in the construction of mines and tunnels in the Fife area. However, following the alleged theft of a lady's handbag on a train to Edinburgh, Slaven appears to have absconded after arrest.

Perhaps he thought Fort William far enough away to avoid detection and maybe a prolonged period without a prison sentence was to his taste? In any event he reappeared in Fort William in 1907 to find the recently opened railway station now serving the town and

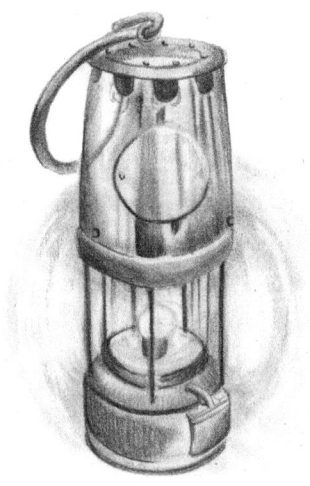

the High Street lit by the country's first electric streetlights. There was a hustle and bustle in the town, the railway had helped bring new employment to the area. Now 52 years of age, he still did not seem to mind the deprivations of the vagrant life. Instead of seeking employment at the Kinlochleven dam works, he joined the group of tinkers, tramps and pedlars that congregated in the High Street, begging and selling items to passers-by.

After more arrests, he would once again disappear. Although he would never return to Fort William, the town would play an unwitting part in his last, great money-making scheme.

The Great War came in 1914 and although Slaven was too old to be conscripted into the army, the work on the coalfields of Fife and Lanarkshire became vital and he was once again able to find employment in the mines. Despite the unforgiving and dangerous nature of the work, Slaven continued to labour in the pits until well into his 60s. Although he was arrested for a drunken fracas in 1923, during which he violently butted and punched another man, his life seemed relatively trouble free. On this occasion he even chose to pay a 60 shillings fine, rather than face the alternative short prison sentence.

Nevertheless, a serious accident in a tunnel in 1926 saw John Slaven seriously injured. He was unable to work in any capacity at the pits and spent six months in hospital. Renting a room in Aberdeen, down to his last 30 shillings, and failing in a claim for the new means tested unemployment benefit, Slaven devised a scheme to ensure he would not need to work again. He took out the following advertisement in the Fife, Dundee and Perthshire newspapers:

Labourers – A few respectable men wanted for work in the Highlands; must pay part fares; accommodation provided. Apply stating nature of previous employment to Agent c/o Wright, 44 Blackfriars Street, Aberdeen.

The mysterious 'Wright' and the address in Aberdeen were, in fact, Slaven's landlady and his own lodgings. The slowdown of the economy had meant the industrial heartland of Scotland was awash with men, unemployed and desperate for work. All willing to travel a long distance to secure employment and all willing to pay their own expenses to get there. To those who replied to the advertisement (and there were a large number) Slaven sent back the following fraudulent letter, from an entirely fictitious company:

<u>The Nevis Construction Company Ltd, Fort William District</u>

Your application is at hand. You are requested to forward 10 shillings part fare, which with your endorsed application, will be despatched to head office, who will send you railway voucher and company's "engaged" card, and also travelling particulars, etc. Wages to commence will be paid at the rate of 1s 2d per hour. Work is rail, road and building construction, and is guaranteed to yield four months' continual employment. You must be prepared to travel within fourteen days, and you are warned not to do so without the company's "engaged" card. It is necessary that you should reply within two days to A. Montgomery, c/o Wright, 44 Blackfrairs St, Aberdeen.

By the end of January 1927 at least 69 men had returned the part train fare to John Slaven. The fraud was a particularly cruel and heartless one, preying on men who were desperate for work – even to the point of paying a portion of their own travel costs. The unlucky men, sadly, never received their 'engaged cards' from The Nevis Construction Company Ltd. Some were so taken in by the matter of fact and realistic tone of the correspondence that they actually travelled all the way to Fort William, convinced that their letter had been delayed in the post, or lost. It is heartbreaking to imagine groups of tired, hungry and disadvantaged workmen arriving at Fort William Railway Station, on a bitterly cold February day, looking for The Nevis Construction Company, only to be met with bewildered expressions from locals, as they earnestly assured them that the company 'must exist, we have received a letter from them'.

Unfortunately for John Slaven, the crime was easily resolved by the authorities. His correspondence address in the advertisements led them straight to him. He had not even had the time to spend his ill-gotten gains. Slaven was tried at Aberdeen Sheriff's Court on February 9th 1927, and entered a plea of guilty. Despite a sound defence in which Slaven's illness and accident were cited as reasons for his desperate actions, Sheriff Laing was in no mood for leniency:

Your fraud was a very cruel and hard one, the people probably sending all the money they had. There is absolutely no excuse. I have no hesitation in sending you to prison for 12 months.

There was not, and never has been, a Nevis Construction Company Ltd in Fort William. Three questions remain unanswered. Firstly, how did Slaven construct such elaborate and convincing letters and did he receive any assistance? Perhaps his landlady was complicit in the fraud? After all, the letters would have been received by her at 44 Blackfriars Street. They also seem to exhibit a style of offence very out of character with John Slaven's previous peccadilloes. At the trial she denied any knowledge or involvement in the offences.

Lastly, why did Slaven choose the name The Nevis Construction Company and why Fort William? Perhaps the name suggested itself to him during the long days and nights spent on the streets begging, looking up at the mountain range behind the town. Possibly he also thought it far enough away that unemployed workers in Fife and Dundee would be unable to check the details. Finally, conceivably, he thought it might be an opportunity to exact a tiny modicum of revenge on a town that had not treated him as sympathetically as he would have wished.

MORAG & LIZZIE

Loch Morar lies west of Fort William. It
separates the traditional district of North Morar
from Arisaig and Moidart. Surrounded by land rising
sharply to 1,500 feet, the loch is more than 11 miles
long, measures more than 1,000 feet in depth at its
deepest point – making it the deepest body of water on
mainland Britain, and perhaps Europe – and contains
more than 81 billion cubic feet of water. The entire
population of the world could be submerged in Loch
Morar – four times over - with room to spare.

The loch itself is home to a mystery of its own. In a
similar vein to Loch Ness (just 40 miles to the east),
Loch Morar could be the location of a large and
prehistoric creature, that could explain the presence
of its more famous cousin. However, the story of the
Loch Morar Monster is actually far more believable,
far more likely and has a host of far more reputable
sightings. Not only are the sightings by more credible
witnesses, the creature has been seen by multiple
witnesses simultaneously, has been documented

regularly over the past 150 years and is backed by trustworthy and logical scientific evidence. Indeed, Adrian Shine (leader of the Loch Ness Expedition for many years) concluded in 2004 that there is far more likely to be a 'monster' in Loch Morar than in Loch Ness.

Why, then, is the story not front-page news? There are two simple reasons.

Firstly, the legend of the Loch Ness Monster is driven by a lucrative tourist industry, boasting two visitors' centres, film appearances, children's books and an avalanche of merchandise. The modern legend of 'Nessie' sprang to life in 1934 with the publication of the 'surgeon's photo', showing the head, neck and body of the creature. This seemingly concrete proof of the monster's existence, taken by a reliable and trustworthy source, has since been proved to be fake. However, this minor inconvenience has been largely ignored by the tens of thousands who visit Loch

Ness every year. Perhaps the idea of two very public monsters, so close together, would somehow dilute the impact of the story?

Secondly, the remoteness and relative inaccessibility of Loch Morar make it a far less worthwhile and lucrative tourist trap. While Loch Ness is bordered by the A82, with easy links to the A9 and airports, Loch Morar is surrounded, not by roads, but by steep hillside and unforgiving terrain. Considering the far fewer numbers of people who witness the splendour of Loch Morar every year, it is even more intriguing and remarkable that so many eyewitness accounts exist. But why do so few of these accounts reach the national media?

The scientific evidence to support the theory of a creature in Loch Morar is compelling. When the great ice cap that covered much of the northern hemisphere retreated, Loch Morar was merely a saltwater extension of the sea. However, an advance by the ice cap 10,000 years ago, in a form of a gigantic glacier, forced a change in the rock formations, cutting Loch Morar off from the sea. Over thousands of years the hundreds of burns that flow into the loch gradually transformed it into a freshwater environment. It is entirely possible that a breeding population of sea living creatures became trapped in the loch and have survived there. The loch is unique. The water never freezes, is not peaty brown like Loch Ness, but is crystal clear with a visibility depth of 80 feet. Beneath its surface live an abundant population of trout, salmon, eel, stickleback and Atlantic char. More than enough to sustain a population of larger piscivores. In fact, recent scientific study has concluded that trout numbers within Loch Morar are inexplicably low, supporting the theory that they may form the diet of a larger predator. Nutrient levels within the water are high too. Not only is the formation of the loch fascinating, its sheer depth surely holds many secrets. Loch Morar is in fact so deep, a person would have to travel 50 miles out into the Atlantic before they could reach such depths. A sobering thought indeed, that a loch in Scotland could be deeper than the sea surrounding it.

So, scientifically the possibility of a large creature existing in the loch seem credible. But what of the witnesses' accounts?

Although the legend of a monster within the loch has existed for many years, the stories are largely mythical. The legend of Morag (or Mhorag) of Loch Morar tells of a mysterious monster that appeared as a harbinger of death – a common tradition in Scottish folklore:

> '*Morag is always seen before a death and before a drowning…there is a creature in Loch Morar and she is called Morag. She is never seen save when one of the hereditary people of the place dies. The Morag is peculiar to Loch Morar. She is seen in broad daylight and by many persons, including church persons. She appears in a black heap or ball slowing and deliberately rising in the water and*

moving along like a boat water-logged. The Morag is much disliked and is called by many uncomplimentary terms.

(Alexander Carmichael, 1902 collection of Highland folklore, uncovered in 2013)

Father Allan Macdonald wrote in 1896/7 that 'The monster that is said to live in Loch Morar has many eyewitnesses… I heard the name of several living witnesses given but I had no opportunity of testing them at first hand.'

In his book *Lochaber in War and Peace,* from 1908, William T Kilgour gathered information from several witnesses of 'unquestionable veracity', one of which claimed to see 'a huge, shapeless, dark mass, rising out of the water like an island.'

The first modern day recorded sighting of Morag appeared in *Tales of the Highlands*, written by James MacDonald in 1887, 'I met the Mhorag one night in January 1887, when crossing the loch to stalk a deer at Raitlan.'

A mention of an encounter with the monster also appears in the novel *The Secret of the Turret* written by Ethel Heddie in 1908. It is worth noting that all these accounts were written and published at least 30 years before the first modern sighting of 'Nessie' and were therefore not a reaction to those – indeed perhaps the opposite is true.

Sightings continued to be reported, often appearing in the American Press. In April 1917 the following article was published in *The Highland News*:

'A monster is still located in Loch Morar. Some places are pointed out where it feeds; the marks of its feet are found at Camus-nam Bràthan; traces of it exist at Ruidh nan Deorcag and Coll-nam-muc. This Loch Morar creature gets from the natives the name 'Morag'. It appears only when one of the natives of the place die ('aon de dhùthchas an aite'). The last time it was seen was in 1898, when Aonghas an Traigh died. 'Morag' is seen in daylight. As its appearance foretells a death, it is called 'Morag Dhubh.'

Morag also appeared in two books published in the USA prior to the appearance of the famous Loch Ness Monster photograph that effectively began the modern-day legend of 'Nessie' and all its related industries.

Sightings of the mysterious creature in Loch Morar continued, all from seemingly reliable sources. Two crofters vanished on a fishing trip on the loch. Although their boat was found, no trace of the men was ever made. A local barman, on a fishing trip, spotted a creature less than 400 yards from his boat. He was able to make out a long, flat neck and head before the animal disappeared underwater. Another resident of Mallaig spotted something in the water, describing it as 'a strange and dark shape, possibly brown in colour.'

There was huge interest and excitement when, in 1948, a party of nine fishermen witnessed the monster. Mr John Gillies, the boatman, had his attention drawn by one of his passengers to an unusual object moving through the water, about 400 yards to their right.

Gillies recalled: "I put the binoculars on it. It appeared to be about 20 feet long, and had five prominent humps. Neither head nor tail was visible. It wasn't travelling fast, about five knots, I would say, and remained several minutes on the surface."

Mr Frank Fleet, one of the passengers, added: "The loch was a calm as a millpond, and we watched the monster for three or four minutes before it disappeared."

John Gillies told newspaper reporters that "I have been familiar with this loch for 24 years, and I have never seen anything like it. I've always been inclined to laugh at monster stories, I am not laughing now."

There were at least 20 further sightings of Morag throughout the 1950s and 1960s. Captain J. Metcalfe, retired from the Royal Navy, and his wife Dora, a computer expert, spotted something close to the surface during the summer of 1966. Seen on several occasions, during their stay at Swordland Lodge, they noted, "It always followed the same track at approximately the same speed of two or three knots."

In 1969 sightings of Morag increased, reaching a dramatic climax during August. Bertie MacLean, a shopkeeper from Mallaig, noticed something under the water whilst out on the loch. It appeared to be twice the length of the boat with four flippers. However, the creature moved away quickly, perhaps disturbed by the presence of MacLean's boat. In July a carpenter from Edinburgh, while on holiday, noticed a 'monster lizard' looking up at him close to the shore in Meoble Bay.

Events took an unexpected twist on 17th August. Two local men, William Simpson and Duncan McDonnell, from Mallaig, decided to take a pleasure trip on Loch Morar in their cabin cruiser. It had been a fine, sunny day and the loch was dead calm. The sun had dipped behind the hills but it was still bright and clear. Their cruiser was approaching the group of islands at the east end of the loch, at a speed of six or seven knots. William Simpson had just lit the portable gas ring in the galley, in order to boil the kettle. Duncan, at the wheel, hearing a noise turned around and spotted something in the water moving quickly towards them in their wake. It caught up with their boat in a matter of seconds. Simpson, returning to the deck, saw it too as it buffeted the side of the vessel:

I couldn't understand what it was at first then I realised – I'd heard stories about the monster. We watched as it came up and it hit the boat and knocked everything over.' Worrying that the flame from the gas ring may have started a fire

Simpson went into the cabin to check. 'When I came out I saw Duncan hitting it with an oar. I was scared – I can't swim – so I grabbed my gun and fired a shot. I don't know if I hit it. I meant to scare it off. I then watched it slowly sink away from the boat and that was the last I seen of it.

The pair felt slightly awkward about the presence of a rifle on board (they had hoped to shoot some deer on a nearby laird's land) and both men agreed not to go public with the story. However, they did tell friends, including John McVarish of the Morar Hotel – who himself had witnessed the monster – and news inevitably reached the press. Soon the story became 'front page news' and the two men returned to the loch in a bid to retrieve the oar with which Duncan McDonnell had fended off the creature. It had been hoped the oar would contain teeth marks that might help identify their attacker. Unfortunately, nothing could be found.

Billy Smart's Circus offered a reward of £5,000 (approximately £75,000 today) for the capture, *alive*, of the monster. The circus intended to make Morag a headline attraction at their Safari Park Lake in Windsor. A spokesman for Billy Smart's said: "We are serious. If nobody can catch this creature for us, we will try to get it ourselves. We are already making enquiries about the best way to catch a monster."

Interest was also attracted from the nearby scientific survey being held at Loch Ness. The Loch Ness Survey team (including Elizabeth Campbell, who would later write the definitive book on the subject *The Search for Morag*) interviewed Simpson and McDonnell, as did television crews from the BBC, Japan, Canada and the USA.

The Loch Ness Survey became the Loch Morar Survey, as a team of 30 observers and scientists, from the University of London, decamped to the shores of Loch Morar for two successive summers. Despite swarms of midges, howling gales, thunderstorms and primitive accommodation, the team bravely stuck to their task throughout the summer of 1970 and 1971. The team set up in a disused, corrugated iron hut (after first chasing out the rats that had set up home there!). Three observation points were set up at Meoble, Swordland and Bracara, each with a tent to sleep in and a tent to protect the camera equipment.

Conditions were challenging although the team was able to observe movement in the water on several occasions. The aptly named Dr Bass spotted a large hump, moving quickly through the water. Two post-graduate students, working on the survey, were leaving the islands in the loch, late in the summer of 1971 and witnessed their boat being tracked by a shape moving in the water, creating a large wake, and matching their speed of 15 knots. Far too fast to be otters or any other known species living in the loch. Elizabeth Campbell was also able to catalogue and quantify all the known sightings of the creature.

The team reported on their survey at a press conference at London Zoo. Morag was left in peace in 1972, as the team did not return. However, the sightings continued.

Duncan McDonnell witnessed the monster again in 1995, whilst out with Donnie Simpson (brother of his companion William, from 1969). They witnessed a large bodied creature hauling itself across the gravel and disappearing into the water. An artist's sketch of their sighting appeared in the *West Word* magazine.

Ewen MacDonald saw three humps moving quickly across the water in 1986 and a party of four girls witnessed the creature in 2002. A tragedy occurred in 2004 when a man fishing in the deepest part of the loch disappeared. His upturned boat was found, his body never was.

After a third Loch Morar Survey operation in 1976 the number of reported sightings had already passed the 200 mark. The majority of viewings being in the remarkably clear shallower waters, usually up to depths of 100 feet or less. This, marine experts believe, adds more credence to the story, as the plentiful shoals of fish inhabit these waters – making ideal feeding grounds for a larger species. Studies of the water content and habitat also revealed that the lower depths of the loch have changed very little and could feasibly support a species trapped there since the loch became separated from the sea. This could also account for the size difference reported in different sightings of the creature. For any species to have survived there, there must be a breeding population, not one solitary animal.

Sightings of the Loch Morar monster continue to this day, yet largely go unreported, while the 'Nessie' industry rumbles on unabated. Elizabeth Campbell concluded after the Loch Morar Survey and the publication of her book on the subject, that the number of sightings was simply 'too impressive to be ignored.'

It might surprise some to find out there is another well documented and mysterious monster believed to be living in Loch Lochy, to the east of Loch Morar. Loch Lochy is also deep, the third deepest in Scotland, 10 miles wide and a half a mile long. Like Loch Morar it is home to yet more mysterious and unexplained sightings. Once again, the sightings pre-date those at Loch Ness and are supported by reliable witness testimony and sound, marine biology.

The expanses of Loch Ness, Morar, Oich and Lochy were all once seawater lochs, until the encroachment of the Second Ice Age cut them off from sea. Over many thousands of years the flow of burns and rivers have transformed them into freshwater lakes. In addition to an average depth of between 250 – 300 feet, there are thought to be huge trenches on the loch floors that possibly extend for depths of up to 2,000 feet – and may well link the lochs in an immense underground network of tunnels. Scientists believe the steep sides of the lochs may also contain huge 'overhang caves', capable of concealing even the largest objects.

In 1929 two local gamekeepers saw what they thought was a large, floating log in Loch Lochy. When they examined it more closely with a telescope, they were able to see that it was actually a large living creature, which they tracked for approximately a mile until it dived below the water. The following year a local man, who lived close to the loch shore, witnessed a strange creature moving through the water. His wife, who was in the habit of washing their clothes in the shallow water at the shore, was promptly advised never to do so again!

On Thursday 29 July 1937, two motorists had a strange encounter along the shores of Loch Lochy. Mr Alexander Henderson and Mr James Anderson, both from Kirkcaldy, described their experience to the Aberdeen Press & Journal;

'We were on our way from Invergarry to Fort William about five o'clock last night', explained Alexander Henderson, *'and drew up to admire the view on Loch Lochyside, about three miles from Laggan Lock, where Loch Lochy is joined to Loch Oich. It was glorious weather, with just a slight ripple on the water. Slowly, fifty to sixty yards out, a curious form came up. What we took to be the body of some sort of beast had distinct undulations. Perhaps hump is a better word to describe them – I counted five.'*

There were two further sightings in 1960, including a photograph showing a dark mass in the middle of a foaming patch of water. During July of the same year Eric Robinson and his family were holidaying near Glen Fintaig when they observed what they first thought was a large wave. However, through binoculars they were able to see that it was a huge, living creature. As it started to move southwards its body appeared to rise up from the water and roll over. The creature's body length appeared to be 15 - 20 feet long, with an estimated overall length of 30 -40 feet. It was dark on top with a lighter underbelly and seemed to have fins on either side. Nine other people also witnessed this phenomenon.

In 1975 Mrs Margaret Sargent, from Fort William, was driving past the loch with her family. At a point close to the Corriegour Hotel they noticed an unusual wake on the otherwise flat and calm loch. A long black shape could be observed moving through the water. She attempted to take a photograph, but the object disappeared below the water.

During the 1980s Mr McGunigal, from Leicestershire, reported witnessing a wake heading towards him, as he was fishing opposite the Letterfinlay Lodge Hotel, on the east side of Loch Lochy. There is an excellent viewing point here and Mr McGunigal was able to see very clearly. He thought it odd as the wake had a distinctive 'V' shape, seeming to indicate that there was something much larger under the water, but not visible – in a similar fashion to that caused by the periscope of a submarine.

However, it wasn't until the 1990s that a flurry of sightings aroused more interest in 'Lizzie', the Loch Lochy Monster. In September 1996, staff at the Letterfinlay Lodge Hotel, which overlooks the loch, saw a strange aquatic monster zig-zagging across the water and both claimed that it was definitely not a fish. They immediately told colleagues and guests and a total of 18 people rushed outside and confirmed witnessing a dolphin-sized creature breaking the surface.

That same summer, while fishing for pike in the loch, local angler Alastair Stevenson encountered a strange creature he thought was approximately 18-feet in length and roughly the shape of an overturned rowboat. The creature reportedly took Stevenson's bait and began to pull the vessel down. Stevenson was quoted as saying, *'I knew immediately it wasn't a pike with that ferocity. I had to stop the line but when I did the power started dragging the boat behind it. All the time I'm thinking it was like a scene from Jaws. Fortunately, my line and rod snapped and that was the end of that. I have no idea what it was, but it was a lot bigger than a pike.'*

This dramatic incident sparked greater interest and an expedition, led by zoologist Cameron Turner, recorded a sonar contact with a large object, close to where the first reported sighting took place. The contact was estimated as being between 18 and 20-

feet in length, and approximately 160 feet below the surface. Two minutes later, after their boat turned sharply starboard in pursuit, a second contact was made, this time at a depth of 200 feet. As their boat approached the centre of the loch, above a deep trench, the objects disappeared. Cameron returned to the loch again in September 1997. On this occasion his team brought an independent researcher and even more sophisticated equipment. They were rewarded with another sonar contact approximately 270 feet below the surface of the loch. For three minutes the team managed to track the signal and were able to obtain clear pictures on their sonar screen.

The father of former Liberal Democrat leader Charles Kennedy was certain that he had unearthed the remains of one of the creatures from Loch Lochy, near the family graveyard in Lochaber. Ian Kennedy revealed he had made the unusual discovery while rebuilding a footbridge to the site of the graveyard at Clunes, near Achnacarry, in preparation for the funeral of his brother Donald;

'When I went to check the graveyard, I found that floods had carried the bridge away', he explained. *'So I set about building a new footbridge. While I was working on the bridge, I found the remains of the skeleton. There was no head and no tail, but the rest of it was 4ft 8 and a half inches long. It has a thick neck, 12 ribs, six horizontal bones from the vertebrae to the pelvis and two hind legs. It has massive two toed feet, with a long talon on the end of each toe, making it*

*look rather like a bird's leg. "But the strange thing about it
is that it has a dorsal fin about three inches high and spiky
bones jutting out about three inches all the way along its back.
I wish I had found the head and tail as it would make it
easier to identify, but I think it's a lizard like creature, called a
Thecodontosaurus. It could well be the monster that was seen
in Loch Lochy. I think it probably swam up from the loch and
came to a sticky end where I found it.'*

Whatever the answer to the mystery surrounding these strange and unexplained sightings, the sheer expanse and depth of the water has made proving the existence – or not – of a surviving prehistoric creature, such as a breeding population of Plesiosaurs, very difficult to confirm. Probably we will never know for certain.

MASSACRE IN A CAVE

In 1814 Sir Walter Scott set sail around the Hebrides, with the aim of collecting material and information for his epic poem *The Lord of the Isle'*. On the Isle of Eigg, Scott managed to find a local guide who showed him the entrance to what appeared to be a small cave, close to the rocky shoreline on the southern coast of the island. The entrance to the cave was covered in undergrowth and difficult to find. It could easily be missed.

Sir Walter Scott crawled into the narrow and low entrance to the cavern, recording later in his journal that the entrance was so small that "one can hardly creep on hands and knees". However, once inside, the roof of the cave rose dramatically in height revealing a huge cavity in the rock. Inside Scott discovered the cave floor was "strewed with the bones of men, women and children, being the sad relics of the ancient inhabitants of the island who were slain."

Despite the trepidations of his suspicious crew, Scott

removed a skull for his collection of 'grim cracks and rarities'. The cave was traditionally known as Uamh Fhraing (St Francis or Frances Cave) – it is now referred to as Massacre Cave. The cave bears witness to one of the most gruesome mass killings in Scottish history.

In 1576 a raiding party of MacLeods from Dunvegan of Skye arrived on a small Island called Eilean Chathastail, just off the coast of Eigg, during a storm. The party helped themselves to the cattle and (it is said) molested the local girls whose job it was to look after the herd. When news reached the furious MacDonald clan on Eigg they immediately rowed across to the island and dealt with the small raiding party. The worst fate was reserved for the first son of the chief of Macleod of Dunvegan by breaking his arms and legs and setting him adrift in a small boat without oars, condemning him to a slow and painful death. It is said that the boat drifted all the way back to Dunvegan on Skye and the chief swore he would have his revenge on the MacDonalds of Eigg.

He despatched a fleet of warriors from Skye, to confront the MacDonalds on Eigg, but their galleys were spotted by a watchman on the cliffs of Eigg, who warned the islanders. Such was the terror among the people of the island, the entire population of 400 hastily made their way across the terrain and hid in the cave. Its narrow entrance was concealed by undergrowth and a small waterfall. An elderly woman, too weak to make the journey, was left behind. It was hoped she could convince the MacLeods that the inhabitants had fled the island by boat.

When the large party of raiders landed they found only the elderly woman who told them she did not know where her fellow islanders were hiding, or even if they were still on the island at all. Searches were carried out for three days but proved to be fruitless. Believing that the MacDonalds had fled the island, the Macleods torched their empty homes before setting sail back to Skye.

After three days cowering in the cave, one of the MacDonald party was sent out of the cave to see if the raiders had left. It had been snowing (which had possibly hindered the MacLeod's search of the island) and, unfortunately, he was spotted against the white cliff by one of the MacLeod ships. The raiding party immediately returned to shore and followed the footprints until they found the entrance to the cave. A stand-off ensued, in which the 400 MacDonalds refused to leave the safety of their hiding place. Members of the MacLeod clan diverted the small waterfall and blocked the entrance to the chamber with thatch and roof timbers. They shouted a warning into the cave that the pile would be set on fire, and everyone inside would surely be killed. However, it seems, at the last minute Macleod of Dunvegan hesitated and decided the Macdonald's fate should be left to the judgement of God. He declared that If the wind blew inland from the sea, he would have the material lit. If the wind blew from the land to the sea, it would not be set alight.

The wind gusted in from the sea. The MacDonalds still refused to come out of hiding, and the bonfire was lit. Once fully ablaze the MacLeods dampened the flames, ensuring billows of thick smoke filled the cave. It was said 395 people died, by smoke inhalation, oxygen deprivation, or from the heat, with only one family escaping to tell the tale.

The events appear almost too horrific to be true. Unfortunately, the evidence seems to support the story of the ordeal, that only one family survived to tell. For many years following the tragedy, remains of the massacre were discovered in the cave. Victorian tourists, including Hugh Miller, the 19th Century geologist, and Sir Walter Scott, all recorded taking bones as gruesome souvenirs from the cave. Eventually concerned islanders pleaded for the remaining bones to be buried in Eigg churchyard and it was hoped that the victims could, at last, rest in peace.

However, in 2016, following a period of natural soil erosion, the discovery of yet more bones was made. The news brought a flock of visitors to the cave during the summer and 53 further human bones were uncovered. This time, the availability of modern scientific methods meant that the remains could be tested to verify the authenticity of the story. Forensic carbon decay dating analysis, by Historic Environment Scotland, was able to prove that the bones did indeed date from the period. The substantial number of bones also seemed to add much credence to the account of events. Further tests also revealed that some of the bones were adult and two were from a child aged nine or ten, seeming to add more weight to the legend.

Sir Walter Scott, who often looked at the skull for inspiration, famously proclaimed, "life is too short for the indulgence of animosity."

This would not be the end to the feud, however. On the first Sunday of May in 1578 a raiding party of MacDonalds from Uist glided silently around Dunvegan Head into Ardmore bay, on the edge of the Waternish peninsula, on the isle of Skye, unnoticed by anyone and bent on vengeance. It was a Sunday morning, and many of the MacLeod clan on the island had gone to worship in Trumpan church. Slowly and silently the MacDonald men gathered around the building and piled brushwood against the door. When the pile was large enough they set it alight, trapping everyone inside the walls of the church.

Suddenly there was a loud shout from the church doors and the worshippers turned around to see the door guarded by armed men, yelling triumphantly. Escape was impossible, everyone in the church was unarmed. The congregation waited, bravely defiant, the women and children terrified. Yet they were powerless against the claymores that guarded the narrow door – their only means of escape. Soon the church began to fill with smoke and flames. Screams from the children filled the building, while outside a lone MacDonald piper played 'wild and scornful music to drown the cries of the dying'. Unseen, however, in the dense smoke, one teenage girl managed to squeeze through a narrow slit in the stone wall at the corner of the church, which served as a window. The gap was so narrow and the stones so rough that she ripped a huge gash across her chest, so horrific that she later died from the wound. It is difficult to imagine the level of sheer terror that enables a person to endure such self-inflicted pain.

She managed to warn the MacLeods in Dunvegan. The men immediately launched a swift and savage counter-attack. The MacDonald's raiding party was outnumbered heavily and slaughtered on the beach, before they could set sail. The tide was so low they were unable to launch their boats across the rocks. Following the slaughter, the corpses of the MacDonalds were dragged off and thrown against the side of a stone and turf dyke wall, whereupon the dyke was simply toppled over the bodies of the dead men. The MacLeod clan deemed the act of burning the church so monstrous that the MacDonald warriors did not deserve a decent burial. It appears that one boat managed to escape, as the MacDonald soldiers fought bravely to the last man against vastly superior numbers.

For many years after the battle, the bones of the dead MacDonalds could be seen protruding between the rocks and earth from the toppled dyke, a gruesome reminder of an awful event. As a result of this, the encounter became known as the *Battle of the Spoiling of the Dyke* (*Blar Milleadh Garaidh* in Gaelic)

The township of Trumpan was never re-established, and the church (now known as Kilconan Church) has remained a ruin, a poignant reminder of another barbarous episode in Scotland's history.

Incredibly though, just 50 years later, and just a few miles across the water in Ardnamurchan another similar massacre would take place.

Mingary Castle, at Kilchoan on the west side of Ardnamurchan, is the westernmost fortification on the British mainland, situated on the westernmost point of mainland Britain. Ardnamurchan belonged to a branch of the MacDonalds called the MacIains of Ardnamurchan. In 1624 the Clan Campbell invaded Ardnamurchan, seizing the MacIain stronghold of Mingary Castle. They immediately garrisoned it and drove the MacIains into hiding in the remote countryside. Some of the fugitives (mainly women and children) sought refuge in a cave on the rocky shore, known as the Cave of the MacIains. The cave lies on the north coast of Ardnamurchan, between the tiny settlement of Ockle and the narrow glen of the Allt Eilagadale, facing out across the steep cliffs to the islands of Eigg, Rum and Muck.

Here the coast is a series of jagged headlands and rocky bays. The cave may well have been the clan's last refuge, a place they retreated to when they were being attacked. It lies at the back of a small bay, cut into the ancient rocks that form the coastline. Although the cave is damp, cramped and cold, it is invisible from the landward side, and very difficult to reach from the rocky beach. The sea in front of the bay is littered with sharp, protruding rocks, protecting it from attack by boat.

It was in this cave that the last of the MacIain women and children were trapped by the marauding Campbells. History does not relate where the men were at the time, though there are suggestions that they had already been caught and defeated on Morvern, to the south of Ardnamurchan, or perhaps they had already escaped by boat, hoping to return for their women and children.

The story of the massacre was passed down through the generations of MacIains, but its truth was at last confirmed in Victorian times, when human bones were excavated from the cave.

The women and children might have survived there due to the cave's remote and obscure location, were it not for the following, disturbing events, as described by Alisdair MacGregor in *The Peat Flame Fire* (a collection of faithfully retold folk stories, compiled in 1937):

They might have remained undetected for a time, had not one of them, weary of his confinement in the dark cavern, come out into the open, and left his footprints in the previous night's fall of snow. It is said that the fugitive, on realising the jeopardy into which he carelessly had thrown himself and his clans-people, endeavoured to cover up his tracks in the snow by retreating backwards toward the cave (giving the impression that someone had left the cave, instead of entering it). In any case, one of the Clan Campbell had observed him, and had hurried off to Mingary Castle, which was now in the possession of his kinsmen. Forthwith a detachment of Campbells reconnoitred the footprints, and traced them to the cave, wherein were huddled several of the Maclains. At the mouth of the cave they kindled a great fire, and thus suffocated its occupants to death. If this incident be true, as well it may be, it occurred just half a century after the somewhat similar incident on the Island of Eigg, when the MacLeods entrapped the MacDonalds in the Cave of St. Frances, and at the entrance to that cave maintained a fire " with unrelenting assiduity," to use Sir Walter Scott's words.

Mingary Castle was abandoned and subsequently fell into ruin and disrepair, until being renovated in 2016, re-opening as a luxury hotel.

GHOSTS IN THE HIGH STREET

The search for the paranormal is usually associated with desolate, eerie battlefields, unnerving graveyards or crumbling castles. When we saunter along our local high street, among the neon signs and the throng of shoppers, we don't expect to encounter a ghostly apparition or sense an unearthly presence.

Until, that is, we take a stroll down the high street in Fort William.

The northern end of Fort William's Victorian High Street was cleared for redevelopment in 1980. The building of a new outdoor centre, shopping precinct and public library required the clearance of, among other things, a huge oak tree that had stood on the site for 200 years. Known locally as 'The Hanging Tree' the mature oak had served as the gallows and had stood just outside the walls of the old Fort. This local landmark had been used by successive governors of the Fort for the execution of Highlanders who had fallen foul of the authorities and of British law.

At the time of the tree's felling, locals shook their heads and foresaw dire consequences. This act of vandalism and desecration, some residents of Fort William warned, would bring with it the Gaelic witchcraft prophecy of 'Buidseachd' (pronounced 'Bootchach') – the curse of ill omen.

Despite the warnings, the library's opening day passed without incident. At closing time, the staff locked the door and left. The following morning they discovered the door appeared to be ajar, however there was no sign of its having been forced open. Books had fallen from shelves, yet the books on either side were undisturbed. Potted plants had fallen to the ground and chairs leant on their side. A one-off incident or a break in? The staff did not think so. Over the weeks and months that followed, a catalogue of unexplained manifestations occurred. None of them could be explained by the staff. An electric typewriter started to print its characters upside down. Objects seemed to have moved places overnight. The staff would leave work in the evening, only to return in the morning to find books on the floor, plants and chairs on their side.

Branch librarian Don McGavin explained: "There have been a lot of strange incidents, with no rational explanation for them." Pens, office stationery and toilet rolls disappeared, then reappeared again – without a staff member being anywhere near at the time. An anorak was left on the back of a chair overnight. When the staff returned the following morning, it was gone. "Nobody ever came back to claim it!", said Don McGavin.

On another occasion a photocopier, although not plugged in, suddenly came to life. The telephone would ring three or four times a day, yet the line was dead. Electrical equipment would malfunction randomly and paintings that formed part of a display came crashing from the wall, although no one was near them at the time.

Librarian Kate Finlay recollected perhaps the strangest episode of all. She found herself being propelled from behind by a mysterious 'unseen force', as she was quite literally pushed out of a room. "It was an unnerving experience", she recalled, "I can't explain it.'" Even more bizarrely staff have heard the sound of a dog, snuffling and panting, inside the building, yet no animal has ever been seen.

Possibly the most ominous incident occurred a decade after the library had opened, and was reported in both the *Daily Express* and *The Press & Journal*. A cable car cabin was displayed outside the library on a 15 feet high steel support (to advertise the ski centre). Overnight it came crashing to the ground, leaving behind a structure that resembled a gibbet or scaffold. "Can it be that the fates are trying to tell us something?", wondered Don McGavin, "the whole thing is quite uncanny."

More recently, in 2009, a French couple took a holiday snapshot outside the library. The pair, Sophie Mager and Remy Ruckey, were not aware of anything unusual when they took the photograph. An eerie white image only appeared when the photograph was processed. Sophie and Remy were not even aware of the stories, nor of the hanging tree, until after the incident. The story, together with the image, was reported widely in the media.

Over the years the ghost has become affectionately known as Jamie, although no one is quite sure why, and even to this day staff have arrived at work and sensed something strange flickering between the rows of bookshelves. The fleeting presence is greeted with a cheery 'Hello Jamie!'

Despite the troubled and turbulent history of the site, the incidents do not appear to be anything more than mischievous in nature – for now, that is!

Take a stroll along the High Street and you will come

to Cameron Square, a compact central point in the town. To the south side of the square sits the West Highland Museum, housed in an imposing Victorian building, originally built in 1835 for the British Linen Bank. The Museum houses a collection of wartime, Jacobite and other local displays among its many rooms.

Both visitors and members of staff have reported the strange feeling that they are being accompanied as they walk along the corridors and between the rooms. The presence does not appear to be unfriendly, however. Many have reported their experiences to newspapers and paranormal databases. Despite the age of the building and the square outside, the ghost is believed to be a relatively recent one - that of curator Edith MacGregor, who passed away in 1969. Staff, working alone in the building, have overheard the sound of an old typewriter on frequent occasions. Yet all the original typewriters were replaced many years ago with computers. Footsteps have also been heard passing along the wooden floorboards upstairs, despite there being no one else in the museum. Staff have even noticed the distinct smell of toast, even though there was no toaster in the building!

A monument to Dr William Kennedy was removed

from Cameron Square in 1965, causing much local consternation. Dr Kennedy died as a result of his courageous help to local sufferers of a typhus outbreak in 1851. A church was also converted for use as a town hall, which in turn burnt down in 1975. Notwithstanding, or perhaps because of, the volatile disruption in the square during the past 50 years, rumours persist that the museum's spectre is that of Edith MacGregor – perhaps disturbed by the constant changes. Edith was born in 1890 and wrote and published *The Story of the Fort of Fort William* in 1954. As well as teaching typing Edith remained curator of the West Highland Museum until her death in 1969.

In 2009 a contractor, working in one of the offices upstairs in the building, heard a voice and began a conversation with a lady he thought was in the adjoining office. When he looked in the room there was no one there. The empty room had been Edith's office.

During 2015 an American tourist, Dundee Warden from Montana, took a photograph of one of the museum's display cases. Although not visible to his naked eye, the image of a ghostly figure appeared to stare back at him from the photograph. The angle of the photograph makes it seem unlikely that the image is merely a reflection. Mr Warden's story was reported in the press and magazines, including *Scottish Field* and several others, in which he explained;

'In my opinion, I do believe this is a ghost. The day I toured the museum I felt as if someone was tagging along with me. The energy felt like an invisible magnet or weight pulling me in a kind of slower motion.'

Perhaps the building works in Cameron Square in 2020 for the new cinema may result in further disturbances and a reoccurrence of unexplained encounters in Fort William's High Street? In the meantime, enjoy your shopping!

THE LAST OUTLAW

Surprisingly, the story of the Last Outlaw in Lochaber is not the tale of a Jacobite fugitive evading the British Redcoats. Instead the story takes place over 50 years after the last Jacobite was hung. In fact, it seems that Ewen MacPhee wasn't prepared to accept the law of any government - English or Scottish.

Ewen (sometimes called Ewan) MacPhee was born in 1786 in the Glengarry area of Lochaber. Around the year 1807, at the start of the Peninsular War against Napoleon's forces, he was conscripted by his laird, MacDonnell of Glengarry, into the British Army (as many young Lochaber men were at that time). While he was stationed at Stirling Castle for training, riots broke out in the local coalfields and the army was called upon to suppress them. MacPhee and others appear to have threatened a mutiny if ordered to use force against the rioters. This may be true as troops from Edinburgh had to be called in to quell the rioters instead.

MacPhee served in Spain during the Peninsular War,

proving to be both an effective and brave soldier, liaising with Spanish guerrillas on behalf of his commanding officers. He rose quickly through the ranks, attaining a position of Sergeant. Unfortunately, MacPhee was unable to read or write and this seemed to severely restrict his chance of any further promotions. He was reported as having been furious on being given this news, believing he had been promised a commission. MacPhee decided to desert the army as soon as an opportunity presented itself.

A unit of men, including MacPhee, was sent on a mission to carry valuable funds to Spanish guerilla fighters in the mountains. The money intended for the Spanish fighters went missing; MacPhee claimed he had hidden it from a possible French search. Whether he intended to return for the money is not known, however, his commanding officer was in no doubt. He immediately had MacPhee arrested and slapped him across the face, accusing him of being a 'Highland dog'. MacPhee was furious and drew his dirk, before he could be clamped in irons, and stabbed the officer, killing him instantly. In a flash he jumped over the wall and ran through the narrow streets of the town. Later, under cover of darkness, he escaped and promptly disappeared, deserting his regiment. MacPhee knew that both crimes would have seen him hung from the gallows.

Managing to evade the authorities for a year, MacPhee eventually made his way back to Lochaber – a journey of more than a thousand miles. Following a tip off, he was arrested in the Glengarry area, while hiding with his sister. MacPhee was handcuffed, marched away by a band of soldiers and taken to a steamer anchored at Corpach. However, while being taken aboard, he slipped free of his bonds, jumped over a precipice and, with musket shots blazing past his head, made his escape once again.

Ewen MacPhee then lived as a fugitive for two years on the remote hillsides around Loch Arkaig, always just managing to evade capture. By 1812 it appears that MacPhee seems to have tired of this existence and decided to settle on an island in the middle of Loch Quoich. where he built a bothy and fortified the island.

He later abducted a 14-year-old girl called Mary, from nearby Glen Dulochan, and together they raised a large family on the island. Their life there seems to be have been relatively untroubled by the law, despite MacPhee making his living largely through poaching, sheep stealing, and selling his own illicit whisky. He threatened to kill any man who dared to cross him and was known to take pot-shots at any Redcoat soldier that came near the island, bellowing that he would never be taken alive. He was a large, fearsome and imposing man, with a shock of red hair and whiskers, who took great delight in wearing full Highland dress, always carrying his dirk and gun. MacPhee became notorious for stealing livestock, and for his temper. He was reputed to have killed his own illegitimate son. Yet he was also consulted by poor local residents, who believed him to be a seer capable of curing their sick cattle.

When English millionaire Edward Ellice purchased the estate in 1830, MacPhee presented himself to the new owner and promptly refused to pay any rent, offering ewe's milk as a gift to the new Laird instead. MacPhee threatened to defend the island to the death if this was not acceptable to the new owner. Despite this unorthodox approach Edward Ellice viewed him as a piece of local colour. MacPhee would often come to the estate and pose in his tartan finery for paintings to be done by visiting guests and artists. These included the Scottish artist RR McIan, who was keen to paint MacPhee for his 1848 book *Gaelic Gatherings, or the Highlanders at Home on Heather, River and Loch*, in which he portrayed aspects of rural life in the Highlands.

It appears that the wealthy Ellice tolerated MacPhee's presence during the summer months when he spent time at his Scottish estate, entertaining such guests as William Gladstone and Sir Edwin Landseer. However, in reality his duties as an MP, governor of the Hudson Bay Company in Canada, and owner of eight sugar cane plantations in the West Indies, probably meant that he spent very little time in Scotland. Alas, it was MacPhee's neighbouring tenants who were forced to endure his temper, volatile behaviour and sheep stealing.

By 1841, MacPhee seems to have cooperated enough with the authorities, that he loathed so much, to complete the Public Census. The 1841 census records him as living on Loch Quoich Island, aged 55, his occupation noted as 'Army Infantry.' His wife Mary is aged 29 at that time and they have six children aged between the ages of three and 13 years living with them, as well as Maryanne McIntyre a 20-year-old 'female servant' and Duncan McIntyre, a 15-year-old 'agricultural labourer'.

MacPhee seems to have become even bolder by 1846, when the *Inverness Courier* carried a story of "the well-known singular outlaw Ewen MacPhee attending a Highland Competition and Sports Gathering" in Fort William, where a crowd of almost 4000 people had gathered. The paper reports that he "left his solitary fastness, to be present at the animating scene, and appeared to be highly delighted with it". He entered the 'Best Dressed' competition for those attired in Highland dress - winning third prize of £1 10s (approximately £200 today).

However, such indulgent tolerance of his outlaw behaviour did not last. Complaints from his neighbour John Cameron, about the extent of his sheep stealing, increased, until in 1850 two Sheriff's officers from Fort William rowed across Loch Quoich to the island to investigate. MacPhee was not at home, but his wife chased off the approaching officers by firing at them, forcing the men to turn and flee the island. Returning a week later in much greater force, the officers found large quantities of tallow and skins on the island - proof of his poaching activities - and arrested MacPhee, who was now aged 64. He was taken away to prison in Fort William. No record of the charges against him remain as he died whilst in captivity from cholera, before ever coming to trial.

It appears that Mary did not stay long on the island following MacPhee's death. The Public Census of 1851 has Mary MacPhee, aged 39, living in Fort William, with her occupation recorded as 'wife of soldier (deserter)'. There are also three further children shown as living with Mary, including her youngest, a baby daughter Ann. Unlike the others, who were born on Loch Quoich, Ann was not, suggesting Mary was probably pregnant when Ewen MacPhee was arrested and died.

Tragically, not long after the Census was recorded, local doctor William Kennedy was called to attend to Mary and her children, after they had become infected during an outbreak of typhus in Fort William. It was reported that Dr Kennedy 'attended to them and cleaned their poverty stricken hovel'. By helping them and saving their lives, the doctor himself contracted typhus and later died. 1,400 people attended his funeral and a statue was erected in his honour in Cameron Square, Fort William.

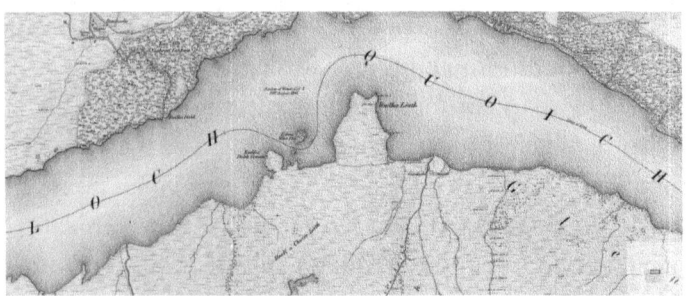
1872 Map of Loch Quoich, showing MacPhee's Island

The island that was the MacPhee family home for 38 years became known as 'Eilean MacPhee' (MacPhee's Island), until it was eventually submerged when the level of Loch Quoich was raised as part of the Garry-Moriston Hydro Electric Scheme during the 1960s, bringing to a conclusion the story of Scotland's last outlaw.

THE FORT WILLIAM HEN

For several years from 1890 until early in 1896 John Turner had made a comfortable living from his poultry holding in Laggan. His hens and ducks could roam freely, pecking the grass outside his cottage and wandering down to the Laggan Burn to drink the cold, fresh water. John Turner often journeyed into Fort William to buy and sell his poultry at market.

1896 saw the opening of the Salen Distillery nearby, and the West Highland Railway brought scores of visitors to the newly electrified Fort William. John Turner rightly hoped that his business might well increase. Queen Victoria had become Britain's longest serving monarch and Glasgow opened its Metro railway.

Yet in Laggan, John Turner's carefully managed poultry business mysteriously started to falter. By October of 1896 his poultry had stopped eating and producing eggs. The hens spent most of the day asleep. Once awake they would not eat until they had visited the Laggan Burn for a drink. Often they fought viciously when they were suddenly awoken, and staggered noticeably across the field. John Turner described their behaviour as 'reprehensible, as if they were under the influence'. Strangely, on a Sunday, the hens and ducks behaved piteously, wandering aimlessly and refusing to drink. Conversely, on a Monday, the poultry were at their worst. Drinking huge amounts from the burn, then cackling loudly and falling asleep for long periods. The hens would often lose their footing and stand on their own eggs, smashing them.

At first John Turner thought that a hen he had purchased in Fort William was to blame. The bird had been sold to him by a soldier from the 92nd Highlanders, who warned Turner that the hen was a 'bit of a character'. It seemed to Turner that this particular hen had been a troublemaker from the start. Before its arrival none of his hens or ducks had drunk from the burn. The Fort William Hen was the first to discover the burn and seemed to have led the rest of the brood there. John Turner decided he would investigate the Laggan Burn. Walking down to the edge of the burn, he noticed a strong smell and a slight discolouration to the babbling waters. He knelt and, cupping his hands, scooped up a handful to sample the oddly coloured liquid.

As he did so, he recognised the taste immediately. Good, strong Scottish whisky! But just how did the burn happen to be contaminated with a stronger spirit than water? A glance upstream gave John Turner his answer – the recently opened Salen Distillery

Company. He soon realised that this would account for the reason his hens behaved differently on Sundays – the only day of the week the distillery was closed.

Armed with this information, John Turner contacted his solicitor and claimed damages against the Salen distillery. Turner claimed that the distillery, "had allowed intoxicating material to flow into the Laggan Burn, thereby causing drunkenness amongst his poultry, consequently rendering them of little, or no value, to him."

John Turner initially claimed £50 in damages, but this was restricted to a maximum of £12 (approximately £1,500 today). The case was heard by Sheriff MacTavish at Oban Sheriff's Court in November 1896 and attracted national attention and a packed courthouse. Salen Distillery defended their case vigorously, claiming the trouble had been caused by the presence of the rogue hen – known in court as 'The Fort William Hen' – who alone had caused the change in the behaviour of John Turner's brood. Defending the distillery, Mr William Scott, solicitor, called for the offending hen to be produced in court – both as an exhibit and as a witness. The Fort William Hen became, probably, the only bird to be questioned in Scottish legal history!

The superintendent of the court brought the offending fowl into the courtroom and the following cross examination took place between the solicitor, John Turner and the Fort William Hen:

Mr William Smith (Solicitor); "Have you ever observed gapes in your hens?" (Gapeworms are a parasite that can cause paralysis and difficulty in breathing in wild and domestic birdlife)

Mr John Turner; "Yes"
Smith; "Have you not considered that your hens are suffering from gapes?"
Turner; "Yes, whisky gapes"
There was laughter in the court. Mr Smith glanced at the hen, then continued his questioning; "Did you know anything about the Fort William Hen before you bought her?"
Turner; "Nothing whatsoever."
Smith; "This is the Fort William Hen, is it? Is it sober?"
Turner; "It is not."
At that moment the hen was prostrate on the bottom of the wickerwork cage, its long neck stretched out through the bars, looking up at the ceiling, crooning to itself.

Turner remarked, "It always sings in that maudlin style when it's far gone."

At this stage in the proceedings the hen seemed to direct some remarks at Sheriff MacTavish, who promptly ordered it to be removed from the court, amid raucous laughter from the gallery. Undaunted, Mr Smith continued his examination, "Was this hen at the distillery burn this morning?"

Turner; "Anyone could see that!". The gallery burst into laughter again.
Smith; "How are the other hens today?"
Turner; "Worse than this one"
Smith; "Was this the only hen you could bring to court today?"
Turner; "Yes, the others were too drunk."
Smith; "So the Fort William hen is not the worst?"
Turner; "That is so - she can hold her drink."
Smith; "What do the hens do when they return from the burn?"
Turner; "Sleep."
Smith; "Anything else?"
Turner; "After a sleep they generally fight."
Smith; "Have you no sober hens at all, then?"
Turner; "Yes, but the drunk ones break their eggs."
Mr Smith, the distillery's solicitor, had probably never had such a difficult day in court. The gallery laughed uncontrollably, and Sheriff MacTavish stated it was the most unusual case he had ever overseen. The distillery's claim that the brood were merely suffering from influenza was laughed out of court and the gallery cheered as John Turner and his prize exhibit left the courtroom.

The High Street outside was packed and the crowd jostled to see the famous Fort William Hen. One thoughtful individual presented it with a half glass of whisky, which the bird drank quickly. This revived it considerably and it cackled loudly, to the intense enjoyment of the bystanders.

The Fort William Hen proved to be a decisive and memorable witness. The Salen Distillery Company fell 'fowl' of the law. Sheriff MacTavish, clearly with his feathers ruffled, ordered the distillery to mend its ways and pay compensation to John Turner. Sadly, no record exists of just how the hens coped with their enforced abstinence (or should that be cold turkey?).

KINLOCHLEVEN
– ESCAPE AND ESPIONAGE

Kinlochleven, nestled in the mountains at the head of Loch Leven where the River Leven flows into the loch, became an important focal point during both the Great War and the Second World War. Firstly, as a prisoner of war camp, and secondly as a secret target for a Nazi mission of espionage. Reminders of the former can still be seen in the village, but details of the second were classified 'top secret' and not declassified by MI5 until recently. Had the mission succeeded however, it might be a very different Kinlochleven that we see today.

Kinlochleven prisoner of war camp (known as Loch Eilde Camp) was part of the British prisoner camp network and initially operated as a satellite to Stobs Camp in the Scottish borders. The facility, built in 1916, was used to house German prisoners of war and detained German nationals living in Britain at the outbreak of the war. Major Andrew Barnard, a veteran of the empire in India, was placed in charge. A nearby camp was also built at Caolasnacon to house some British conscientious objectors.

The camp at Kinlochleven held some 1000 German prisoners. They were housed in 13 huts along with the usual ancillary buildings, laundry rooms, washrooms and latrines, kitchen, theatre, workshops and a hospital. The guards and officers were housed in a separate area overlooking the general campsite. There was a parade ground, a detention block, sergeants' mess and officers' quarters. The nearby railway line was used to bring in supplies for the camp and sometimes to take the guards and prisoners into Kinlochleven. Despite the Geneva Convention specifying that prisoners were not to be used for manual labour vital to that country's war effort, it was deemed that projects in and around Kinlochleven did not meet that criteria, and large parties of the men were put to work. The prisoners were mainly used in the construction of an aqueduct, bringing water from the Blackwater dam to the aluminium smelter, and in the construction of the first road into Kinlochleven from Glencoe, running through the hills on the south side of the loch. Trusted interns were also put to work in the village and in constructing parts of their own camp.

The prisoners were well treated by the villagers and, in return, helped maintain their houses. Men working on the new road construction were given whisky by the locals and even temporarily housed when their camp was flooded in a severe storm. "The German prisoners were accepted into the community as sons of German parents - who had been conscripted into the war – just like our own sons, fathers, uncles and cousins were", reported local historian Avril Watt, "the German prisoners were looked after as our own."

Yet, despite their treatment and distance from the horrors of the trenches in France and Belgium, the camp was not without incident or escape attempts. One prisoner died, during the violent storm that flooded the camp, when a timber beam was dislodged and smashed into his head. Another was shot and killed whilst trying to escape. However, on Tuesday 15th August 1917 two men did manage to escape, while working as part of the gang on the new road. They eluded capture by heading into the trees and under cover of dark attempted to make their way across Glencoe and Rannoch Moor. Scotland Yard issued a description of the two men and newspapers across the country carried the story of the men's escape and their description:

ESCAPE OF GERMAN PRISONERS

Scotland Yard announces the escape from the working party at Kinlochleven General Camp of Karl Konig and Daniel Schneider, prisoners of war. They were both locksmiths by trade. Konig, aged 23, complexion bronzed, hair brown, eyes blue, medium build, height 5ft. 8in., brown corduroy trousers, complete suit of oilskins with official blue patch. Schneider, aged 37, complexion speckled, hair fair, eyes grey, build average, height 5ft. 10in., dressed as Konig.

However, a night on Rannoch Moor proved too much for the men and they were arrested close to Kinloch Rannoch the following day by Police Constable Craig of the Perthshire Constabulary. He reported that the escapees did not resist arrest, had no provisions and were 'fed up'. They were taken by train to Perth where they served six months' imprisonment before being returned to camp.

The remains of the prisoner of war camp can still be seen today. Although overgrown, some of the base pillars, concrete foundations and retaining walls are still visible.

Recently declassified MI5 files regarding the interrogation of a high-ranking German intelligence officer, revealed for the first time a secret Nazi plan to use Irish nationalists to attack the aluminium smelter at Kinlochleven.

The story of *Operation Seagull* (as the plan was codenamed) began in November 1941, at Friesack POW camp in the Brandenburg region of Germany. Here, many captured Irish soldiers from the British army were interned. The Abwehr, Nazi Germany's Intelligence service, believed they could be 'turned' and persuaded to take part in sabotage operations against Britain.

However, the Germans' recruitment drive produced disappointingly few volunteers. Only 10 of the men were judged to have sufficient potential as saboteurs. Among them a young corporal from County Tipperary, Andrew Walsh, and a Royal Irish Fusilier from Roscommon called James Brady. Walsh had been serving with the British Expeditionary Force in France in 1940 when he was captured as the Germans overran his unit, while Brady, who joined the Fusiliers in 1938, had fallen into the Nazis' hands weeks after the Germans invaded the island of Guernsey, where he had been imprisoned for a drunken attack on a policeman.

The small group of 10 men were taken to an Abwehr camp in Stettin for initial training, where they met Dr Kurt Haller, a former lawyer and now head of the Abwehr counter espionage department, responsible for special missions in Ireland and Britain. Dr Haller soon singled out Walsh and Brady as the most promising of the group. In an interrogation carried out by MI5 after the German surrender in 1945, Dr Haller gave his first impressions of the two Irishmen.

Andrew Walsh he described as "mature, determined and quiet, seeming to have genuine Irish nationalist feelings, to which was added an adventurous streak."

Brady, in his opinion, was "a strong Irish nationalist, who claimed to have contacts in IRA circles".

Once satisfied that both men were capable of undertaking dangerous sabotage operations within the British Isles, Haller now had to decide on a suitable mission to assign each man.

Brady, it was decided, was to be dropped in Northern Ireland and find employment in the Harland & Wolff shipyard in Belfast. There he was to recruit four or five sub-agents (IRA members if possible) and undertake small-scale sabotage in the shipyard. For Walsh, Dr Haller has something altogether more ambitious in mind: "The target selected for Walsh was chosen by the German Air Force," he revealed under interrogation, "he was to interrupt production in an aluminium works near Fort William in Scotland."

Opened in 1909, the aluminium works at Kinlochleven, 16 miles from Fort William, was an essential component of Britain's war machine, producing almost all of the country's aluminium. As such, it had been designated a priority target by the Luftwaffe, who had previously attempted to bomb the facility on 13th May 1941. Nazi propaganda broadcasts by Lord Haw Haw had hailed the raid a major success, however the truth was very different. The German bombers failed to release their payload on the target as the mountains in the vicinity of the aluminium works interfered with the planes' bombing run.

In desperation, the Luftwaffe turned to the Abwehr to put the Kinlochleven factory out of action. Dr Haller had made a study of the facility and understood that the plant's Achilles heel was the 8 mile-long pipeline connecting it to the Blackwater dam, which powered the factory. Walsh was ordered to destroy the water pipes leading to the electricity plant with special explosives. If he failed to achieve this, he was given a secondary target - a smaller power plant in the vicinity, also connected with the aluminium works.

In the summer of 1942, Walsh, Brady and several of the other Irish volunteers were taken to another Abwehr training camp, known as 'the Quenztgut'. Here they were assigned their codenames 'Vickers' (Walsh) and 'Metzger' (Brady), and put through an intensive training course, receiving instruction in the use of radios, secret codes and explosives.

Walsh was then informed that his target was to be the Kinlochleven aluminium factory. He accepted the mission and was told he would receive up to 25 Reichsmarks per day in payment for his mission. Walsh, Brady and the other Irishmen were then sent back to Stettin Training Camp while Dr Haller awaited final approval of the plan from the Abwehr's chief, Admiral Wilhelm Canaris.

Finally in September 1942 Operation Seagull was given the go-ahead and Haller made the final arrangements.

Walsh was to be dropped by parachute near to Glasgow, where he would rendezvous with other German agents. He was then given his false ID papers in the name of Thomas Dunphy.

The Irishman was also given £8,000 in cash as payment for undertaking the mission, although the money was undoubtedly counterfeit (this was a common tactic employed by the German Secret Service when paying their own agents). The men were then taken to an airfield near Trondheim in Norway, from where Walsh and Brady were to be flown to Scotland and Northern Ireland, respectively.

Walsh waited in his room at the secret Luftwaffe base near Trondheim, while the ground crew carried out its final inspection of the Focke-Wulf 200 Condor, the aircraft which in a few hours' time would take him on his secret mission to Scotland. However, as he nervously pondered the dangers of his impending mission to Scotland, he was interrupted by a harsh knock on the door. He answered it, and was confronted by his German 'handler' Dr Kurt Haller, flanked by several armed Gestapo officers, who arrested him on suspicion of treason against the Reich.

Operation Seagull, the only major sabotage raid the Nazis planned to carry out in Scotland, had been scuppered. Not by the British, but by the very man entrusted by the Germans to carry it out. Only minutes before his departure Dr Haller had received a telephone call from his superiors in Berlin, ordering him to arrest the Irishmen immediately.

Throughout his months of training, Walsh had been hiding a secret.

The evening before leaving for Norway, Walsh had confided to another of the Irish volunteers, Thomas 'Red' Cushing, that he had absolutely no intention of carrying out his sabotage mission. Instead he had planned to surrender to the police as soon as he had landed in Scotland. Unfortunately for the two men, the Gestapo, who were unsure of the true loyalties of their Irish agents, had bugged their conversation.

With the reliability of the Irishmen clearly in doubt, *Operation Seagull* was scrapped. Brady and Walsh were taken back to Germany under armed guard. Walsh was sent to Sachsenhausen concentration camp. He managed to survive the war and was handed over to the British when the camp was liberated in 1945. No charges were brought against him.

Brady managed to convince Haller of his loyalty and he eventually joined an SS unit. After the war he spent a year on the run in West Germany before finally surrendering to the British. Little is known of what happened to Andrew Walsh after the war. He returned to Ireland and, it is thought, died in 2009.

Kinlochleven emerged relatively unscathed from the war. The aluminium smelter survived intact. Had it been destroyed, Britain's war efforts would have been severely impaired and the community we see today may have been transformed into a very different place.

THE FORT WILLIAM FIRES

In the six-year period between 1929 and 1935, a series of unexplained fires took place in and around Fort William. All were sudden and all mysterious.

During the second week of February 1929 several inexplicable fires erupted across the north west of Scotland, from Oban to Inverness. On Saturday 16th February residents in Fort William awoke to find the 'Cowhill', that rises immediately behind the town, ablaze. Almost the entire hillside, which rises over 900 feet above the town, was engulfed in a roaring mass of flames, from the upper Auchintore Road to the boundary of the Forestry Commission land to the east. Police, the fire brigade and local volunteers rushed to help quell the flames, as they threatened a nearby explosive storage dump, belonging to the Lochaber Water Power Works. Beaters worked frantically to stop the flames spreading as fears spread that an evacuation might be needed. Fortunately the threat was averted, but only at the cost of the loss of many young trees planted by the Forestry Commission. Mr Edward

Malcolm, factor for the estate of Lady Fairfax-Lucy of Glen Nevis, could only look on as acre upon acre of land was destroyed. Even as night fell, the beaters and police worked on, the fire visible for miles around. Only by two o'clock the following morning was the blaze brought under control and residents could sleep more easily in their beds. By dawn, the hillside presented a bleak and blackened appearance to the inhabitants of Fort William, covering hundreds of acres.

No reason or cause could be found for the cause of the fire which was all the more unusual for taking such hold in winter.

On 31st May in the same year, there was an explosion and fire at the oil store in Fort William, operated by the contractors for the Lochaber Water Power Scheme. The explosion and fire caused a burning barrel of petroleum to explode. Lachlan Mackenzie was so badly wounded he died the following day in hospital. His family attempted to sue the contractors, Balfour Beatty & Co Ltd, for the sum of £400 claiming that not enough adequate care had been taken to ensure the safety of its employees. The family also argued that the contractors offered no insurance cover to compensate dependents of victims in such circumstances (also see the chapter *Monessie Camp*). Balfour Beatty countered the accusations by reminding the court that the pursuer in this case, "did not take certain measures to prevent or reduce to a minimum the risk of the store going on fire, and to enable such a fire to be controlled and extinguished." In 1929 there was no legal obligation for an employer to provide any sort of insurance to cover their employees – no matter how dangerous the work.

On the 8th June 1930, the last mechanic to leave Messrs Mcintyre & Sons garage, at Auchintore, Fort William, locked the doors and secured the premises for the night. Everything was still and calm. Yet, in the early hours of the following morning, a neighbour was awoken by the smell of burning. Rushing to the window they saw the premises ablaze and immediately raised the alarm. The fire brigade arrived promptly. However the building was already a raging inferno. Seeing that it was impossible to save the garage, or the motor cars stored inside, the fire brigade concentrated on preventing the blaze from reaching the neighbouring school and houses, as well as the entire fleet of buses used on the Fort William to Inverness bus route. This was achieved but the garage was destroyed, along with valuable tools and machinery, and £6,000 worth of motor cars. Automobiles were an expensive luxury in 1930, and the collection (of which only part was covered by insurance) would be worth in the region of £400,000 today. No reason or culprit could be found for the fire.

On the shores of Loch Linnhe, about ten miles from Fort William, sits the vast Conaglen Estate, running to 40,000 acres. The estate and house were purchased by the Earl of Morton from the Macleans of Ardgour in 1858. During the afternoon of 23rd March 1931, the present Earl and Countess of Morton were preparing to leave for Edinburgh, when they were alerted by cries from the staff. A fire had begun in one of the rooms of

Conaglen House. The fire brigade and staff battled for five hours to bring the fire under control, until finally the flames were extinguished. There was severe damage to the house however, the sitting room and two other rooms were destroyed.

Although an electrical connection was suspected, examiners were unable to definitively name the cause. The fire had been sudden, unexpected and had taken hold very quickly. Conaglen House is now fully restored and offers luxury holiday accommodation.

In January of 1932 fire broke out in farm buildings at Tirandrish, close to Spean Bridge. The blaze seemed to originate in a barn with a slated roof and open sides, used for the storage of hay. At the time of the fire the barn contained around 100 tons of hay. The flames soon took hold and the adjoining house and farm buildings were soon under threat. Dr Drysdale, the owner, telephoned the Fort William fire brigade. However, the buildings, it seems, sat just outside their jurisdiction. Unable to persuade them to help, Dr Drysdale quickly rounded up local volunteers and helpers who battled to bring the blaze under control. Eventually, and without the help of the fire brigade, they managed to control the inferno, but not until at least £1,000 worth of damage was caused and the building completely destroyed. No clue could be found to explain the outbreak.

The Fort William area, it seems, was gratefully free of such occurrences for three years, until 1935 when once again the town was involved in dramatic incidents. Mrs

MacDougall from Inverlochy Village was turned into a human inferno when her paraffin stove caught fire and exploded, while she was preparing a meal. Her family bravely doused the flames and she was rushed to Belford Hospital. Despite suffering severe burns and shocking injuries, incredibly Mrs MacDougall survived. Again, experts could not ascertain a reason for the sudden ignition of the stove.

The fire brigade was called into service again in November, this time at Fort William Pier, when a fire started on board the three-masted Danish schooner *Clytia* which was carrying a cargo of barley destined for the distilleries. Unfortunately, after putting out the small fire, it was observed that the ship had collided with the harbour wall and was beginning to ship water. Fire crews laboured all night to pump water from the vessel and to save the valuable cargo of barley. Eventually the fire was brought under control, the ship saved and at least some of the cargo saved.

The final fire, in this unusual rash of incidents, came during the same month, when further conflagrations broke out in newly planted Forestry Commision land at Leanachan, near Spean Bridge. Another large area of tree planting was destroyed and although the fire brigade investigated, no cause could be found.

And with that, the strange sequence of fires came to an abrupt end. For the most part, the incidents remain unsolved.

THE APPIN MURDER

Just seven years after the tumultuous Jacobite Rising of 1745, with tensions still running high, the murder of Colin Roy Campbell of Glenure took place in Lettermore Wood, on the south side of Loch Linnhe, close to Kentallen. The murder would lead to a trial and a miscarriage of justice, still considered by many in Scotland to be one of the worst in Scottish legal history.

Colin Roy Campbell, aged 44, was the Crown appointed factor on the forfeited estates of Ardsheal, Callert and a portion of Lochiel. On 14th May 1752 Colin Campbell (also known as 'Red Fox') was en route to Lochaber to carry out evictions of Stewart tenants in the area. One of his travelling companions and kinsmen, Mungo Campbell, would later provide in court an account of the events that led to his murder. The party were on horseback, travelling through Lettermore Wood, on the south side of Loch Linnhe. As the track became too narrow to accommodate two horses riding abreast, Colin Campbell rode behind

Mungo. Suddenly, Mungo heard a gunshot and turned around to find Campbell had been shot. Although Mungo would later tell the court that he had caught a brief glimpse of the assailant, he was only able to recall his dark brown coat as the man disappeared into the trees.

Despite attempts to fetch medical attention, in the form of surgeon Patrick Campbell, efforts to save Colin Campbell were futile. He died shortly after. The surgeon was able to ascertain that the victim had been shot twice in the back. The entry wounds were less than three inches apart, indicating that either a musket rifle had been used, or that possibly two musket balls had been loaded in a pistol and fired simultaneously. In either case, the murderer must have been in close proximity. Both bullets had passed through his body, severely damaging Campbell's liver.

An immediate proclamation was issued by the authorities, offering a reward of £100 (approximately £20,000 today) for the capture of the assassin. In the murder of Campbell, the British government saw a potential danger from Jacobite rebels to all of their agents in the Highlands.

Alan Stewart (sometimes called Alan 'Breck' Stewart

due to his pockmarked face – a legacy of smallpox) was widely considered to be the prime suspect. He had previously publicly threatened Colin Campbell and had enquired about his schedule on the day in question. A warrant was immediately issued for his arrest. However, he fled and managed to evade capture. His story would eventually become part of the novel *Kidnapped* by Robert Louis Stevenson.

Unable to trace Alan Breck Stewart, James Stewart (known as 'Seumas a' Ghlinne' – 'James of the Glen') was next to attract the authorities' attention. He and the deceased had previously engaged in public disputes (despite working together). Stewart had claimed Colin Campbell was 'no friend of his' and that he carried out his business with a 'high hand'. It had been rumoured that Colin Campbell had dispossessed James Stewart of the Glen of Glenduror Farm – the best in the district – and replaced him there with his own cousin. This seemed reason enough to suspect him. Despite having a strong alibi at the time of the murder, corroborated by witnesses, James Stewart was arrested.

Immediately following the murder, the case attracted widespread public and political attention. The Lord Justice Clerk Charles Areskine wrote to the Earl of Holderness, the Secretary of State, in London, assuring him that a wide ranging enquiry would be made in order that the "barbarous wretches, actors and accomplices of this assassination may be discovered and exemplarily punished".

From the very beginning of the legal proceedings the odds were stacked against James Stewart. His trial was held before the Western Circuit Court at Inveraray - a Campbell stronghold – and not the High Court in Edinburgh, which would have been far more appropriate for such a high-profile case. In addition, 11 of the 15 jurors appointed in his case had the surname Campbell and the presiding judge was Archibald Campbell, the Third Duke of Argyll, and Chief of Clan Campbell. The trial started at 5 o'clock in the morning and did not break for 50 hours! Stewart was indicted and convicted of "being guilty airts and pairts" of the murder. 'Airts and pairts' being an old Scottish legal expression meaning an accessory, an aider and abetter. The principal suspect in the crime, Alan Breck Stewart, was never found, allegedly escaping to France.

James Stewart was incarcerated at Inveraray, awaiting execution. Whilst in his cell he received news that Captain Grahame, a seafarer and a courageous fighter, had planned a scheme to break Stewart out of jail in the dead of night. The plan may well have worked, however the authorities moved him to a more secure cell in Fort William garrison to await his fate. While waiting in his cell there, he received news of a further cunning escape plan. A party of 50 men would be used to snatch James Stewart from the scaffold, on the very day of his execution. A map and plan detailing the proposed course of action was shown to James Stewart. However, he bravely refused and forbade anyone to attempt his rescue. Stewart knew that as well as risking their own lives, the raiding party would be risking reprisals against their families and friends.

On 7th November, James Stewart was escorted by three companies of soldiers (totalling 100 men) to Ballachullish in Appin, on the south side of Loch Linnhe. The government took no chances. Troops occupied the ferry, on both sides of the loch, and all the small boats close by. Soldiers lined the approach roads from Glencoe on one side and the Strath of Appin on the other. Even so, a posse, gathered from the men of the Macleans of Ardgour, and the Camerons of Nether Lochaber, had mingled among the thronging crowds, hoping for a chance to affect a rescue. However, they were poorly armed and realised it was hopeless.

James Stewart was to be executed upon a specially constructed gibbet to be erected on a 'conspicuous eminence' above the narrows at Ballachulish (near what is now the south entrance to the Ballachulish Bridge). He died protesting his innocence and recited the 35th Psalm before mounting the scaffold; "False witnesses rose; to my charge things I not knew they laid. They, to the spoiling of my soul, me ill for good repaid."

To this day in the Highlands, it remains known as 'The Psalm of James of the Glens'.

A letter appeared in the London newspapers soon after, written by a witness to the execution:

FORT WILLIAM NOVEMBER 9th
I was present yesterday at James Stuart's execution, who behaved with great decency and resolution. He read a paper, which he afterwards signed and delivered to the Sheriff, containing a long narration of facts, and denying, in the most solemn manner, his accession to, or knowledge of Mr Campbell of Glenure's murder, or being concerned in the said murder he suffered.

His body was subsequently hung in chains on the same spot. The location was deliberately chosen due to its proximity to the scene of the murder and to nearby Ballachullish – James Stewart's home. Political tensions and a strong public feeling of injustice surrounded the case, largely due to a general uneasiness over the trial and the guilty verdict. It was decreed that Stewart's gibbeted body was to be guarded by 16 men from the command outpost at Appin. The military guard built a hut at the scene and his decaying corpse was continually guarded until April 1754. In January 1755, it was reported to the High Court that the remains had blown down in a storm, but the Lord Justice Clerk ordered it to be speedily hung up again before the news spread and attempts could be made to bury the body.

It was clear, from the very outset of the trial, that the proceedings, execution, and subsequent public display of the body, were very much a political statement. Lord Holderness, the Secretary of State in London, wrote to the Lord Advocate, obviously pleased with the outcome of James Stewart's conviction:

Nothing could be more material to the future wellbeing and governing of distant parts of Scotland. The exemplary punishment of this notorious criminal would convince those previously misled that hitherto the only true and solid happiness was founded on His Majesty's authority and protection.

Although the authorities may have been satisfied with the verdict of the trial, the cost of the proceedings to the public exchequer may have raised some eyebrows, although it does show the determination of the government to obtain a result in the matter. The total cost to the Treasury was £1,334 9s 2d (approximately £287,000 today) – including £255 (£55,000 now) for the cost of entertaining the Sheriffs of Argyll and Inverness-shire!

Some years after the execution the decomposed body of James Stewart was taken down from the gibbet and secretly buried in the chapel of Keil, close to Duror, situated on the shore of Loch Linnhe. A monument was erected there in 1911 poignantly stating that James Stewart was executed 'for a crime of which he was not guilty'.

There has been much written and said about the case since 1752. Both the character of Alan Breck Stewart and James Stewart appear in Robert Louis Stevenson's *'Kidnapped'*.

In 2001, Anda Penman, an 89-year-old descendant of the Clan Chiefs of the Stewarts of Appin, revealed what she alleged to be a long-held family secret. She said the murder was planned by four young Stewart lairds without the sanction of James Stewart. The four young men held a shooting contest between themselves and the assassination was committed by the best marksman among the four, Donald Stewart of Ballachulish. According to other stories, Donald desperately wanted to turn himself in, rather than allow James to hang and had to be physically held down to prevent this. Several years after James's execution, when the body was finally delivered to the Stewart Clan for burial, Donald Stewart of Ballachulish was responsible for washing the bones before the funeral. Interestingly, Donald Stewart's name had been previously mentioned as a strong suspect in the case, notably in *The Book of Balcardine*, written by Alexander Campbell Fraser in 1936.

As recently as 2008, a Glasgow lawyer John Macaulay asked the Scottish Criminal Cases Review Commission to reconsider the case on legal grounds, following his meticulous study of the trial transcripts which showed there was 'not a shred of evidence' against Stewart.

His plea was rejected on the basis that the case was too old to be in the interest of justice.

SMUGGLERS AND GAUGERS

Lochaber and the West of Scotland was a veritable hotbed of smuggling in the early years of the 18th century. Perhaps more so than anywhere else in Britain.

Following the union with England in 1707, Scotland found itself subject to stringent new rules and regulations regarding trade and taxes. New customs and excise officials were appointed, all trained to more stringent English standards. A new Customs House was built at Fort William, to supervise the sea as far south as Tarbert. Even after the threat of another Jacobite rebellion subsided, a garrison of soldiers was kept at Fort William until 1854 to help deter smuggling.

The new regulations, tariffs, and the presence of customs officials were all deeply resented by the inhabitants of Lochaber.

The West coast of Scotland was well placed for trade, with its easy access to the open sea, its abundant natural resources of timber and slate (which could be shipped easily to the lowlands), and its relative proximity to Ireland. There were ample opportunities to avoid tariffs, in both directions, and to 'cock a snook' at the authorities simultaneously. Merchants could earn a small fortune by avoiding excise duty, and it also made them popular with locals too. The poorer among the community could buy their goods more cheaply and, as a result, landowners knew the rents due to them were more likely to be paid. Everyone seemed to benefit – except for His Majesty's Revenue Service of course.

Unlike the more land-locked regions of central Scotland, where small, private illegal whisky stills were the most common form of smuggling, Lochaber bore witness to a large scale and highly profitable smuggling trade by sea, operating for many years and for a wide number of different products. Even today a number of footpaths still carry names such as 'Smuggler's Path', telling us of their original purpose.

Ships from Glasgow and Oban docked at Fort William (some to unload and some before onward journeys). Manifests would be altered to show the true tonnage of the cargo. In 1732, the *Betty* was chartered by William Kirkpatrick, a merchant, to carry a substantial cargo of provisions from Londonderry to Norway. The ship instead sold all its cargo to the owners of the Strontian lead mines, who urgently needed meal and other foodstuffs for the large number of miners and their families. It was illegal to import goods from Ireland under the terms of the union with England. This time, however, the excise officers lay in wait and the hoard was seized by Collector McNeil and his men.

Ships laden with goods (often tobacco, on which tax was high) would leave Glasgow or Greenock en route for Fort William. However, on arrival there was often 10-20% of the cargo missing. Confused customs officials would alter the manifest documents, assuming there had been an administrative error. However, an unscheduled stop en route at Horseshoe Bay, near Oban, gave a well organised smuggling operation the chance to offload as many as 3,000 hogsheads of tobacco (A hogshead was a large, wooden barrel capable of holding up to a thousand pounds of tobacco).

During the 1790s a farmer called Andrew MacDonald lived on the island of Eilean Shona in Loch Moidart. He was fondly remembered as one of the most daring smugglers to operate on Scotland's West coast. MacDonald was a seaman of some renown and frequently outmanoeuvred the boats belonging to the customs officers. On one occasion he shipped an illicit cargo from the Faroe Islands to Loch Boisdale on South Uist. Shortly after reaching the port his crew spotted a revenue cutter boat appear in the port. Cool as ice, Andrew MacDonald told his crew to go about their work on the deck as if nothing had happened. Sure enough, the cutter pulled alongside. Immediately the revenue officer demanded to know exactly the type of cargo he was carrying. To this MacDonald promptly replied, "the very best, made up of silks, gin, brandy and tobacco, not an article of which duty had been paid on". He then added, "you should come over and seize it without a moment's delay." The response from the customs officials to MacDonald's outrageous bluff was laughter and smiles. As they sailed away, the chief customs officer shouted some advice, "Your saucy tongue will be better bridled when you do have something to conceal!"

Another west coast smuggler was Black Ranald, a native of Eigg. On one occasion, when being hotly pursued by a revenue cutter boat, he sought refuge in Loch Moidart. He ran his vessel into a narrow creek opposite Eilean Shona, on the Ardnamurchan side. Quickly he lowered his masts and the revenue crew sailed straight past without noticing, assuming Ranard had travelled further up the loch. Once they were out of sight, he hoisted his masts and sails and made for the open sea.

On another occasion his ship was boarded in the calm waters just off the point of Ardnamurchan. This time, instead of surrendering, his crew fought hand-to-hand with the officers. Black Ranald and his men overpowered the officers, threw their weapons in the sea and unceremoniously dumped the men adrift in a small boat. He became a wanted man following this incident and was forced into hiding. Unfortunately, he had a brother who was mistaken for him and arrested at Greenock. Ranald's brother protested his innocence and resisted arrest strenuously. During the struggle he was badly wounded and died from his injuries.

Loch Moidart was widely used by smugglers for the

arrival of illicit supplies of barley from Uist and Tiree. In an effort to counter this trade the government stationed customs officials at Eignaig and Briaig, which had the effect of largely putting the smugglers out of business.

Whisky was, of course, the most frequent and most profitable contraband to be smuggled in Lochaber. The word 'smuggling' has two meanings in Scotland. Both the illegal trade in goods, to avoid taxation, and the illegal manufacture of spirits (usually whisky) to avoid the payment of duty.

Women were frequently used to smuggle whisky along the footpaths that crisscrossed the region. Often, they would be used to surprise the excise officials (or gaugers, as they were known), by hitting them with sticks while the men conversed with them! Women could also be used to carry huge 'belly canteens' under their garments, simulating pregnancy and thus throwing the gaugers off the scent. One particular female smuggler, walking from Laggan with a concealed jar of whisky, was stopped on the road by a customs officer. He removed the offending jar, but as he did so the woman cried out; "Oh, I am nearly fainting, give me just one mouthful out of the jar." The unsuspecting officer allowed her the desired mouthful, which she cleverly squirted into his eyes, and she escaped with the jar before the officer recovered his sight and presence of mind.

The Rev W Mason Inglis wrote a journal, during the 1890s, in which he recounted some of the tactics and dodges employed by the smugglers:

In the days of the Scottish smuggling the running of the whisky from the bothies in the mountains of Lochaber, where it was taken to the villages and towns, to be sold, was conducted on an extensive scale. The favourite routes were the old cattledrove roads, sheep-tracks, and the least frequented hill roads. Many long miles were travelled with the precious burdens, and many risks and hardships encountered for its sake. The ankers (a container holding about 35 litres) *were slung over the backs of hardy little ponies – each one tied to the tail of the one in front – under armed escort marching along paths where only the most sure footed creatures could hold their way.*

The smugglers from Lochaber had sympathisers and confederates everywhere, and they were welcomed at every public house.

Smugglers were treated with greater consideration than ordinary prisoners. They were often incarcerated at Dingwall jail, which was less oppressive than some Scottish prisons. The offence of smuggling was not considered a heinous one, and they were not regarded as criminals. Offenders were often allowed home from Dingwall jail on Sundays, and for some special occasions, and they usually returned to continue their sentence. Imprisonment for illicit distillation was regarded neither as a disgrace, nor as much of a punishment. One West coast smuggler is said to have suggested to the Governor of the Dingwall jail the starting of smuggling operations in prison, and that he would be happy to undertake the distillation if the utensils and materials could be found. Very frequently smugglers would borrow money to pay their fines, then began work immediately to repay the debt.

A frequently told story tells of smugglers having their casks of whisky forcibly taken from them by the 'gaugers', who would then take the cask to their rooms at the inn for the night, before returning to the Customs House on the following day. During the evening the smugglers would pay the girl delivering the gaugers' food to their room, to report the exact location of the cask within the room. They would then carefully drill a hole through the ceiling from the floor below and remove the evidence. When the gaugers awoke the following morning, the cask would be empty! This seems to have happened on many occasions, in many localities, with several inns still claiming to have an 'auger' hole in their ceilings!

An incident of a more sinister nature ended fatally around 1820, approximately ten miles northwest of Spean Bridge. Customs officers carried out a raid on buildings lying to the south of the River Glass, where they discovered a large quantity of malt concealed in a barn, which the smugglers were determined to defend. The smugglers crowded behind the door, which was of wicker-work to prevent it from being forced open by the gaugers. Unable to force the door, one of the officers ran his cutlass through the wicker-work, and stabbed one of the smugglers, Ian Mor, in the chest.

Fearing that serious injury had been done, the officers hastened away, but, in their haste, one of them fell over a bank, and was captured by the angry smugglers who severely trampled, kicked and beat him. He was conveyed to the nearest inn but unfortunately died the following day. Ian Mor, who would live a long life, proudly showed the scar of the wound on his chest to a retiring customs official almost 80 years later in 1900!

Changes to the tax charged on whisky production took place in 1787. Duty was levied at 20 shillings per gallon capacity in the Highlands and at 30 shillings in the Lowlands. The differential in favour of the Highlands was to compensate for the poor natural resources and high transport costs of the region. To offset any unfair advantage over Lowland distillers, transportation of Highland whisky across the line became illegal, as were stills below 40 gallons in size. Thus, in a single stroke, many small distillers were outlawed, and what had been a popular home industry was now prohibited.

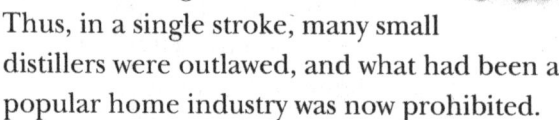

Further increases in the tax on malt and distilling licences in the 1790s made illegal manufacture of whisky even more favourable and profitable. Indeed by 1820 as many as 14,000 illegal stills were being confiscated in Scotland every year, with more than half the whisky consumed in the country being done so without the taxman taking his cut!

The Excise Act in 1823, which sanctioned the distilling of whisky for a licence fee of £10, did have the effect of reducing the number of illegal distillers. In fact many legal, and still existing, distilleries were set up on the site of previously illegal operations. One man who thought it still profitable to carry on his illicit trade was the notorious Ewen MacPhee (his story is dealt with in the chapter *The Last Outlaw*). Ewen operated several stills in the remote hills around Loch Quoich. He was very careful, only burning oak as it gave off less smoke. During the winter months he would sit for days watching the drips of liquid slowly distilling, rather than depart and risk leaving footprints in the snow.

As he grew older, and customers became harder to find, he devised another cunning plan to profit from his smuggling activities. One day he removed his usual garb of full Highland dress, attired himself as a simple cottar (farm labourer), and walked boldly into the office of the Excisemen at the Fort William garrison. Despite there being an outstanding warrant for his arrest, the gaugers did not recognise him. MacPhee promptly asked if there was a reward on offer to anyone that could show the authorities the location of an illegal still.

The Chief Customs Officer answered: 'Aye there is, old man, five pounds for each, or a flogging and a spell in jail, if you try to mislead us. And remember we want the equipment, not just a place once used for the illegal trade.'

'I will show you three stills that belong to that bandit MacPhee', Macphee told them.

With that, he led six armed gaugers on horseback into Glengarry, where he showed them three whisky stills he had abandoned. With glee the exciseman smashed the equipment to pieces, taking the evidence away with them. MacPhee was handed his reward and he promptly left, leaving the gaugers eagerly guarding the three locations in the hope that they might catch the great outlaw Ewen MacPhee!

By 1850 it had been hoped that the smuggling of whisky had all but died out in Lochaber. However, a rash of incidents soon showed this was otherwise. Customs official Mr Thomas Fleming and two of his cuttermen (excisemen who worked on patrol boats) were searching in the hills of Inveroy and stumbled upon a smuggling bothy in full operation. The smugglers were busy mashing the grain and did not notice the gaugers until they were about to enter the building. In a flash, the offenders turned and ran, through an escape hole at the back, leaving all their equipment behind. Two of the officials gave chase and the third stayed behind to destroy, or seize, all the equipment. More than three hundred gallons of whisky were poured away and a still, mash-tun and ground malt were transported to Fort William. Meanwhile, despite a spirited effort to apprehend the smugglers on the hillside, they managed to evade capture.

Perhaps looking for an easier target, the excisemen

made a grave error in June 1852. Mr Meyrick Bankes, a wealthy businessman and the High Sheriff of Lancashire, was in the habit of sailing his yacht from his English estate to his summer residence in Letterewe, on Loch Maree. Scarcely had he dropped anchor in Poolewe Bay than his yacht was boarded by a gang of customs officers, who proceeded to impound his vessel and seize everything on board, charging him with smuggling. In a fury of rage Meyrick Bankes sued the Customs and Excise Office and even had the matter raised in parliament. Needless to say, the red-faced officials returned his property intact, claiming it was all a misunderstanding! The newspapers gleefully reported that 'smuggling whisky to the Highlands was like shipping coal to Newcastle!'

The authorities decided to draft in an experienced and feared customs officer named Donald MacDonald, who had previously thwarted the efforts of illicit operators in Caithness. In 1856 a large group of officers, led by Donald MacDonald, searched the hills of Locharkaig for 12 days, convinced that an illegal stilling operation was taking place there. Finally, at the Farm of Clunns, they discovered a large manufacturing facility including a malt kiln, a large quantity of whisky and wine, and a grinding mill fixed to a tree. The entire facility was torched, and the distillers were fined £30 (approximately £3,000 today).

A sophisticated smuggling operation was thwarted in 1857 by Donald MacDonald and his team. While searching at the Rocks of Craignanach they discovered, in a hidden cave, a large malt mill, fly wheel and copper still. All the items were destroyed or removed but the smugglers were lucky on this occasion and escaped. Donald MacDonald, buoyed by his successes, became convinced there were illicit operations taking place on the many small islands nestling in the middle of the River Treig, in the Braes of Lochaber. Despite previous failures to uncover any smuggling in the area, he plunged into the ice cold and rain swollen river and, ignoring his own safety, swam across to one of the islands. He was rewarded with the discovery of a large copper still and other apparatus which had been cunningly attached to rope and lowered into the river in order to conceal it.

Thanks in part to the efforts of Donald MacDonald the business of illegal distillation did reduce in Lochaber, at least until his retirement. Word must have then spread, as smuggling increased again in the 1880s. In 1882 the Fort William and Fort Augustus Customs Service were forced to combine their efforts to uncover a cunning smuggling operation organised by a crofter named Donald Campbell in the hamlet of Murlaggen. Their attempts were thwarted later that same year, however, when their efforts to make a seizure

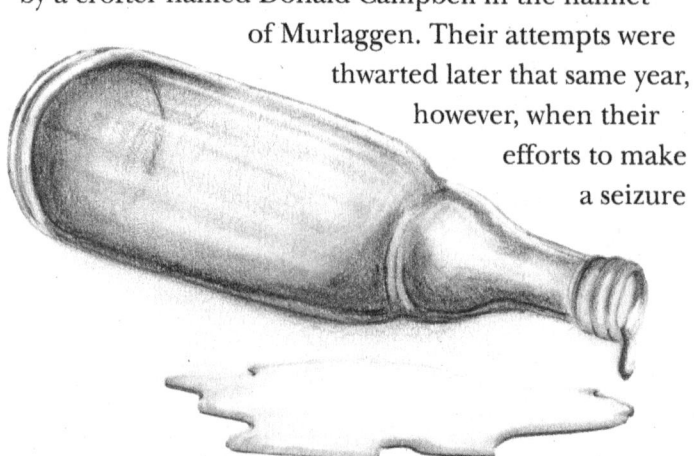

were stopped by a party of six men with blackened faces. The gaugers realised that discretion was the better part of valour and withdrew immediately!

Illicit whisky production reduced greatly in the 1900s, as many men (tired of the large fines and being forced to distill outside in freezing conditions) took employment in the burgeoning and legitimate whisky industry. Although cases of smuggling were still reported, they became the exception, rather than the rule.

We cannot, however, finish this chapter without mentioning the most important, valuable and high-profile cargo to ever be smuggled out of Lochaber. It was not whisky, tobacco or provisions, but a man – Bonnie Prince Charlie.

Following defeat at the Battle of Culloden the Bonnie Prince fled across Scotland, as the British Government forces pursued him relentlessly. Supporters hid the Prince from the Redcoats for five months until he could reach Loch nan Uamh on the west coast in Lochaber. Thanks to the help of a Jacobite supporter, Flora McDonald, he was taken across to Skye in April 1746 disguised as Betty Burke, an Irish spinning maid. The escape has entered legend however, when he was nearly discovered as he unthinkingly hoisted up his skirts to cross a river.

Despite a staggering reward being offered by the British Government of £30,000 (more than £6.5 million today) not a single Scotsman or woman revealed his location to the Redcoats. Bonnie Prince Charlie was eventually able to escape to France from the shores of Loch nan Uamh in Lochaber on 20th September 1746 – from the same spot in which he had first landed on 25th July 1745 to raise the Jacobite Standard.

His escape has been immortalised in the folk tradition as the *Skye Boat Song* written over a century later and still played today.

> *'Speed, bonnie boat, like a bird on the wing,*
> *Onward! the sailors cry;*
> *Carry the lad that's born to be King*
> *Over the sea to Skye.'*

THE GREY DOG OF MEOBLE

AN CU GLAS MHEOBAIL

The threat to the British Empire, posed by the French Revolution of 1794, saw the British army join forces with Bourbon Spain and Portugal to fight Napoleon's troops for control of the Iberian Peninsula. Many Scots were called away to join regiments fighting the campaign, and although the young men who journeyed from the Highlands were not experienced soldiers, they were known for their skill on horseback and their courage.

In the remote crofting community of Meoble, nestled in the hills between Fort William and Mallaig, close to Loch Morar, lived a young man called Dugald MacDonald, son of a local landowner. Dugald owned a large Scottish deerhound and was extremely attached to the animal. The female dog was striking in appearance due to her size and beautiful grey coat. Like so many other young Highlanders Dugald was called to fight, joining probably the 92nd Highlanders or the Scots Greys, and went away to take part in the Peninsular Wars, leaving behind his much loved and faithful deerhound.

When Dugald returned home, several years later, his neighbours informed him that his beloved dog had left home and was living wild on an island in the middle of a small and remote hill loch. During his time away the dog had also given birth to four pups. Dugald was warned that, due to their lack of human contact, the dogs were now completely feral. The pups were almost fully grown and were so savage it was dangerous to go anywhere near the island. Dugald desperately wanted to be reunited with his beloved dog and, ignoring the warnings, set off for the remote spot. The only way to reach the island was to swim across the loch. Dugald did this and managed to locate the dogs' lair among the thick heather and peaty undergrowth. His old deerhound was away, looking for food, but the pups heard him approach and emerged to savagely tear his body to pieces. The deerhound returned to find the bloody scene and, realising it was her old master, howled loudly in agony. Her continual wailing brought the crofters from the glen to the scene. The pups were swiftly hunted down and killed and Dugald's body was removed to be buried in the small graveyard at the mouth of the Meoble River.

Legend tells us that the creature maintained a lonely and pathetic vigil at her master's grave for many years, in all weathers. She frequently woke the neighbours with her loud and mournful howling, crying out for her master. Finally, the glen became silent as the dog passed away. Her body was discovered stretched out beside her master's grave, where she had vainly spent her last few years of life.

For several years the story was often spoken of in the remote community until gradually, with the inevitable passage of time, it slipped from memory.

However, several years later, one of Dugald's brothers fell seriously ill at his cottage in Rifern, a small crofting hamlet lying just across the river from Dugald's grave. One night the ghost of the deerhound appeared at his bedside. The dog looked at him for several minutes, then let out an anguished howl and vanished. The Grey Dog of Meoble had been unmistakeable to Dugald's brother. He died shortly afterwards. Much talk followed among the crofting communities in the region – it was the first sighting of the ghost of Dugald's deerhound. Could it be a premonition of death, a commonly held belief in the Highlands?

Stories and legends about the grey dog spread among members of the South Morar MacDonald clan. Many members of the clan reported sightings of the ghostly, shaggy-haired apparition, always appearing just before the death of a family member. Many of the MacDonald clan emigrated to Nova Scotia and the legend spread, with sightings of the deerhound reported there too.

A well-known and respected Highland writer, named Carald nan Gaidheal, recorded incidents of sightings before his death in 1862. The legend seems to have spread, not only to Nova Scotia, but to other parts of Scotland too. Sightings also included members of the MacDougall family, a branch of the MacDonald clan. The grey dog tradition first appearance in writing seems to be in a manuscript of folklore by Father Allan MacDonald, written in 1896. A Morar fisherman named James MacDonald published his notes on the grey dog in *Tales of the Highlands, by a Mod Medallist* in 1907. James MacDonald, in his notes, tells us the deerhound's name was Elasaid. One of only two known copies of this extremely rare book is kept in the Heritage Centre in Mallaig.

A rare Gaelic manuscript, detailing Canadian tales of the grey dog legend, is held in the Sruth nan Gaidheal collection of the St Francis Xavier University library in Cape Breton, Nova Scotia.

Perhaps the best documented sighting, however, of the ghostly deerhound occurred in the early 1900s in Glasgow. An old lady, whose family were originally MacDonalds from Meoble, lived alone in a city tenement and had been confined to bed for many years. A neighbour friend from across the street was in the habit of calling on her every day to attend to her needs.

On one occasion, as the neighbour was leaving, a large grey dog passed her on the stairs. She had never seen the hound before and thought no more about it until, much to her surprise, she saw the dog again the next day. In this instance the dog was lying on the old lady's doorstep. With some difficulty she pushed the dog aside and went in. When the neighbour mentioned the strange and unusual dog in conversation, the old lady sat up in bed, her eyes wide open. She asked her neighbour to describe the animal; "It was very large, around the size of a Shetland pony, it was grey with a long curly tail". "Ah", exclaimed the old lady with a smile on her lips, "the faithful friend – she has come at last."

With that, she sank back down into her bedsheets and passed away peacefully.

During the 1950s a large grey dog was seen lying in the front hall of a well-known Oban hotel. None of the guests at the hotel seemed to own the dog, or had any knowledge of who did, so the manager asked the hall porter to put the dog out. The porter did this, on several occasions, however the dog continued to return. On the evening of the last known sighting of the animal the hall porter was found dead in his room. He too, it was later discovered, was a MacDonald of Meoble.

The legend is still known in the Morar district and locals think of the Grey Dog of Meoble as 'a ghostly creature akin to a she-wolf – heard and even seen on stormy nights.'

The story has a more recent twist, however. In 1982, well respected local journalist Iain Thornber determined to find the island and trace the origins of the story. In some versions of the original story the legendary isle in the middle of the loch is named as Eilean Allmha, in Loch Morar. However, Thornber's research showed that locals in the surrounding hamlets and communities identified the spot as a nameless isle in a remote lochan named Tain Mhic Dhughaill ('the Little Lake of MacDougall's cattle'). The area is remote and barely visited. Mysteriously, on a detailed 1876 Ordnance Survey map the lochan was originally named Feith a Mhath-ghambaa (loosely translated as 'bog of the fine young heifer'). Its name appears to have changed at some point around the time of the publication of the first account of the Grey Dog of Meoble.

The hamlet of Meoble is largely abandoned and sits in a remote area roughly a mile from the southern shore of Loch Morar. Dugald MacDonald's body is still reputed to be buried in the long abandoned, and almost unrecognisable, graveyard.

Iain Thornber decided to make the journey to Tain Mhic Dhughaill. His arduous trek to the barely visited isle, seemingly untouched by human hands, was made on foot, across rough ground, at least a mile from the nearest mountain path and even further from the nearest road. Finally he reached the spot on New Year's Eve and instantly realised he had found the legendary home of the Grey Dog of Meoble. In the shadow of Sgurr na Plaide, on the north shore of Loch Beoraid stood the small lochan with the unearthly isle dominating it. Dark in colour and contrasted by the frozen, mirror like lochan, the isle was indeed a sinister and unworldly place. Iain Thornber gingerly, and bravely, walked across the ice of the bleak and frozen lochan to the isle where Dugald MacDonald had met his fate. The isle's dark colour, which added to its mysterious appearance, was immediately obvious. It was almost entirely made of dark peat and covered in thick heather. Iain Thornber was probably the first person to walk onto the isle in many years, and may well have been the last.

It was a brilliantly bright and clear day, perfect for photography, so Thornber decided to capture an image of the isle and lochan for his 1982 article in the *Scots Magazine.* However, the photo was found to be flawed. Despite near perfect photographic conditions, the image displayed an uncanny blue grey tinge. Iain Thornber remarked that he never encountered anything of a similar nature, either before or since. He contacted the film manufacturers, who confirmed there was no fault with the film, but were stumped and completely unable to explain the strange tinge to the photograph.

Iain Thornber remarked; "Had the Grey Dog been closer to me than I imagined? Perhaps. It is said that in this part of the Gaelic speaking world, the veil of the intangible is easily parted."

MONESSIE CAMP

During the 1920s the Lochaber Water Power Works offered work to a large number of men, as construction began in the hills on a hydro-electric scheme to provide power for the new aluminium smelting plant in Fort William. The work was uncompromising and tough – and so were the men employed to do it. Balfour Beatty and other contractors drafted in a large labour force, usually dubbed navvies or gangers. The conditions were dangerous, cold and difficult. Often men were laid off, only to find themselves miles from home without funds, family or friends. Workers were housed in camps especially erected for the purpose.

Close to the River Spean in the Monessie gorge sat one of the workers' camps, which became known as Monessie Camp. Rudimentary at best, the camps were often nicknamed 'shanty towns' by the men. Untreated water from Dugh Lochan, a small loch 1,000 feet from the camp, was regarded to be adequate for its use. The water was pumped by an electrically-driven pump, installed at the lochan's edge. Wooden huts, a temporary bridge and powerhouse were built (the landowner would not allow anything more permanent on the site). One of the few comforts afforded to the men was a visit to the hotel bars in Fort William, Roy Bridge or Spean Bridge, on a Friday or a Saturday night, to spend their hard-earned wages.

During the 1920s and early 1930s at least 72 men died during construction works, resulting from such causes as explosions, electrocution, falling rocks and carbon monoxide poisoning. Modern health and safety regulations simply did not exist. Whilst, for the most part, the deaths were examined, they did not result in thorough police examinations or legal procedures as would be the case today. Tempers often frayed and fights between the Irish and Scottish workers frequently broke out. There was a high dependency on alcohol among the 'gangers'. Many had also fought in the Great War, just a decade earlier, and still suffered nightmares and delayed 'shell-shock' from their experiences. The sound of gelignite and the confines of the tunnels and shafts reminded them, all too vividly, of the bombs and trenches.

In April 1928 Patrick Carr, a driller from County Donegal, fell 110 feet down a shaft and was killed. Two months later Patrick Carbin, a 40-year-old married driller also from Ireland, died when scaffolding collapsed on him. William Byrne, a labourer from County Wexford was electrocuted at Number 1 intake tunnel in the same month. The deaths were not investigated. John Cuthbertson (a 36 year-old married man) was found with a crushed skull in 1928, drowned in a burn, between camp Number 8 and camp Number 9. The incident was recorded as an unfortunate accident. Hugh Comiskey, a 24 year-old sanitary worker from Glasgow, was found suffocated to death in his bed at Number 1 camp on 6th June 1926. His death was recorded as 'asphyxia due to suffocation', but no record of a formal investigation exists. In May of 1928 David Forsyth, an electrical engineer from Roy Bridge, working on the power scheme, was found dead with a fracture to the base of his skull. No reason could be found for the injury.

By an unfortunate stroke of bad luck two members of the same family were killed within one month of each other, between December 1931 and January 1932, both in the same horrific way. Both Hugh and James Gallagher were killed when they accidently drilled through old pieces of gelignite left on the floor in Laggan tunnel. The behaviour and treatment of the volatile explosive gelignite in the freezing conditions seems – by modern standards – to be scarcely believable. James Loughan from Cambuslang was killed by an explosion in December 1925, when instructed to thaw out a batch of gelignite by warming it up! James Garrety was perhaps even more unlucky.

He became one of the first victims of the harsh working conditions, when a roof collapsed on him at Monessie tunnel during his first day of work in 1925. He had only arrived on site the previous night.

The uncompromising conditions, coupled with the cold, the frequent accidents, and the unpleasant reminders of the recent war, also had an acute effect on the ganger's mental wellbeing. Caesar Lusardi, a pipeline erector, was due to be sent to a mental institution on 19th June 1928. However, he went missing from the camp. Lusardi's body was eventually found on 15th July by a ghillie, employed on the Inverlochy Estate, drowned in the River Lochy at Dalnacarry. The body was barely recognisable.

The 15th July was a sombre day for the workers employed on the hydro power scheme. On the same day that Caesar Lusardi's body was discovered another worker, walking back to the camp, spotted a strange looking parcel lying in a ditch beside the road near Torlundy Farm. He retrieved the package, and to his horror discovered it was the body of a newborn baby, wrapped in cotton, and badly decomposed. He wept openly. The body was never identified.

John MacLeod, a popular ganger from Inverlochy, was found at Corrie Lees, Ben Nevis, in October 1925. He had committed suicide by shooting himself twice with a rifle. One can only imagine his suffering as he realised he had not succeeded in killing himself with the first shot, then pulled the trigger for a second time.

Richard Neagle, an ex-soldier suffering from shell-shock, hung himself from a tree behind Ben Nevis Distillery in the summer of 1928. He had never recovered fully from the Great War and, even a decade later, could not reconcile his experiences.

The tragic accidents and fatalities did not confine themselves to just the gangers, however. John Kelly, a senior concrete inspector, succumbed to the effects of alcoholism in 1925, and William Thomson, the engineer-in-charge, from Kinlochleven, fell into Roughburn Dam while crossing a temporary bridge.

The influx of workmen at Monessie Camp brought with it a crime that had not reared its head since the invention of the motor car. A century previously, before the existence of a police force, it was a common occurrence to be robbed at the roadside. The crime, known as Highway Robbery, seemed to have all but died out with the increasing number of motor cars on the roads, and the installation of the first telephone lines, which helped the police to respond more quickly to incidents. However, the depression of the 1920s and the influx of workers to the Lochaber Water Power Scheme saw an increased number of robberies take place.

John McVinish, a joiner from Inverness working on the site, appeared at Fort William Courthouse in June 1925 charged with Highway Robbery. McVinish had assaulted another workman and robbed him of his pocket-book containing £14 (more than £800 today). He pled guilty to the attack and, with numerous other offences taken into account, was sentenced to three months' imprisonment with hard labour.

Robberies continued for several months and the gangers were warned to be extra vigilant when out after dark, especially when they encountered workmen who had been recently laid off. In November 1925 Alex MacKay was returning to the camp after nightfall:

Along with a number of mates', he explained, *'I had not long left the hotel at Roy Bridge when, in an isolated part of the road, we heard someone call for help several times. Thinking it was a colleague in trouble, I said to the man with whom I was walking that I would go back and see what was wrong. He urged me not to do so, as he thought the whole affair looked like a plan.*

However, I decided to go back and when near the spot from which I imagined the call came I shouted out "Is there anyone there?". The words were not well out of mouth when I was seized from behind by a man, who caught me by the neck and tried to garrotte me. As I was struggling a second man caught my arms and I was eventually thrown to the ground. As I lay on the ground, I heard one of the men say "boot him!". Following this I received a kick to the chin, which rendered me half senseless for a moment. As my mind cleared, I felt someone going through my pockets.

Alex MacKay was robbed of 18 shillings, four bottles of beer and some candles for the camp. Luckily he had been able to make out his assailants by the glow from their lit cigarettes and was able to describe them to the camp boss and the Fort William police. As a result John Robertson and Edward MacDermott received prison sentences with hard labour. The men had recently been laid off from the camp and had become increasingly desperate.

One ganger took matters into his own hands. One evening, during October 1925, John Cornwallis was walking from Monessie Camp towards Roy Bridge. His 17 year-old sister was walking with him, although she was slightly in front. As she passed around the bend in the road, and temporarily out of his sight, John heard a scream and a cry for help. He quickly ran around the bend in the road and came upon his sister being accosted by four rough and violent looking men. Two of the men were holding his sister, while the other two were attempting to molest her. She was struggling and screaming. Unfortunately for the 'ruffians' (as they were described later in court), John Cornwallis was a boxer of some repute, who had fought for both the army and the police in the ring. His boxing record was excellent. However, the odds were against him. The four men attacked John with bottles and at least one knife, but he more than held his own, landing severe blows on his assailants. During the struggle he suffered several cuts and bruises but managed to distract the men while his sister was able to break free and run for help. The police and several of John's workmates were able to arrive in time to see John landing punch after punch. They stepped in and the men were promptly arrested.

After the attack the men appeared at Fort William courthouse. John, and his colleagues, were acclaimed heroes and the hard working and brave men employed on the Lochaber Water Power Scheme could hold their heads up high once more.

MALLAIG MYSTERIES

Mallaig, a small fishing port and settlement on the west coast of Scotland, derives its name from the Viking *'Mel Vik'*, meaning bay of the sand dunes. The area thrived thanks to the fishing industry, the arrival of the West Highland Railway, and its ferry links to the islands.

The quiet community, tucked away in the north west of Lochaber, has three unusual and intriguing little mysteries of its own. Not hidden away in the depths of time, but all occurring relatively recently.

Ships and ferries leave from Mallaig on a regular basis. However none seem to be have attracted as much trouble as the *Merchant Vessel (MV) Lochmor*. Built on the Clyde in 1930, for David MacBrayne Ltd, the *Lochmor* began service as a mail steamer, car and passenger ferry from Mallaig as part of the Outer Islands Service. With a gross tonnage of 542 tonnes, and 49 metres in length, the *Lochmor* could carry up to 400 passengers.

Despite being newly built, the steamer found itself aground on rocks and in difficulty in rough seas, off the coast of Lochaber, on several occasions between 1930 and 1939. Perversely, whenever the vessel was most needed, to carry supplies to the islands, it foundered. The *Lochmor* almost managed its moment of glory in January 1934 when she frantically steamed against storm force winds and currents in answer to a distress call. The captain of the *Lochmor* received this urgent distress call from the Finnish steamer *Vicia Ketka*, via the Malin Head wireless station:

Vicia Ketka, position latitude 57.41 degrees north, longitude 7.0 west; engine trouble, drifting against Neist Point on Skye Island; requires immediate assistance.

The Lochmor radio operator responded immediately; "Lochmor proceeding to her assistance; expects reach her in 40 minutes."

With that, Captain Donald 'Squeaky' Robertson ordered the steamer to head at her full speed of 12 knots towards the dangerous and sheer cliff face and rocks around the Neist Point Lighthouse on Skye. The ship battled its way, buffeted and beaten, towards the south west coast of Skye, past the Aird of Sleat and Soay. As the *Lochmor* reached Neist Point, amid the gloom of the cold, January night they could not locate the *Vicia Ketka*, nor any sign of any wreckage. Worrying that the Finnish steamer had gone down with all hands, the captain ordered the *Lochmor's* wireless operator to radio Malin Head. Fearing the worst, they waited with bated breath as the reply came back:

Vicia (as previously reported) begins: At 8.30pm engines repaired; now proceeding under own steam.

The *Lochmor* had risked life and limb on a pointless journey. With that it limped back to Mallaig, no doubt with a furious skipper. Known locally for his quick wit and sharp tongue, even Captain Robertson might have been rendered speechless! Perhaps it was with this incident in mind that he nonchalantly kept his ship and crew overnight at Armadale so that they could enjoy a local wedding. A furious telegram came within hours from head office; "What holds Lochmor at Armadale?" He sent back the cool reply: "Two ropes – one at each end."

Following a relatively uneventful war, in which the *Lochmor's* most dangerous cargo was sheep on their way to market, the steamer became involved in an intriguing mystery in 1949. Police were called to the dockside at Mallaig on the morning of Saturday 18th June, by worried shore radio operators from MacBrayne's ferries. They had no explanation for a string of mysterious messages picked up from the *Lochmor* during the night.

The first message read; "SOS Operator going to be murdered. Now off Mallaig." The next came 20 minutes later; "I think that certain persons are after me. Want help." An hour later a final message was received; "Captain says send police to Mallaig. We are an hour away."

The police arrived and promptly boarded the *Lochmor* as she pulled dockside in Mallaig. Strangely, they found everything in order. There was no commotion on board and the crew were going about their business in the usual manner. The ship's owners said later that the wireless operator had been taken ill, and that there had never been any trouble on board. The operator was taken to hospital and the ship returned to work. No reason was ever given, and the matter was never investigated properly. When asked for more explanation by the police the ship's owners merely replied that there had never been any trouble between the crew and that the captain was completely unaware of the bizarre events of that night.

In November of that same year the Outer Hebrides were battered by a week of raging gales, in which winds reached speeds of up to 100 miles per hour. Twelve passengers and all the crew were marooned aboard the *Lochmor* for 36 hours while the ship lay against rocks, unable to move and unreachable by any outside help. Finally, the winds abated and the ship could return to Mallaig harbour.

In November 1952 the steamer became stranded on flat rock, below the water's surface, as she made for the pier at Lochboisdale on South Uist. No one could explain why the ship had run aground on a journey it had made on many previous occasions. Being just a few yards from the pier, it was easy to disembark all the passengers. The captain, however, stayed aboard and the ship was refloated on the next high tide.

A year later, in December 1953, the *Lochmor* was asked to assist the islanders on North Uist, when the island faced a shortage of bread and fuel. By 1st December, all supplies of bread and petrol on the island were exhausted. Frantic and worried residents sent protest telegrams to the offices of MacBrayne's, to their local MP and to the Minister of Transport. 'Where was the *Lochmor*?', they demanded. The answer came back – eventually – as islanders began to ration their own supplies, the ship was lying in Mallaig Harbour with engine trouble.

Time was running out for the *Lochmor*. New hoist-loading car ferries were being phased in for the Outer Island Service. These could load and offload vehicles far more quickly and could better cater for the growing tourist trade to the Scottish Islands. Before the *M.V. Lochmor* could be replaced (scheduled for 1964), the ship was involved in one more small mystery. In good weather and calm seas, in June 1962, the *Lochmor* sent out an urgent distress signal, which was picked up by the Malin Head Station; "Send Mallaig lifeboat. Aground at Kilmory Point, Isle of Rum."

The lifeboat was despatched, and a passing Royal Navy mooring vessel also answered the call. The ship was rescued and the reason for its running aground could not be fathomed in such calm seas and familiar waters. It was to be the end of the line for the *Lochmor* however. It was sold in 1964 to a Greek shipping firm and finished its years in the Mediterranean before eventually being scrapped and broken up in 1984.

Another absorbing mystery occurred in August 1938. Police in Mallaig received a call from two yachtsmen. The men had been sailed inland from Soay, on the south side of the Isle of Skye, and moored in the bay by the island of Eilean Glas. They then hiked their way inland on foot, following a footpath next to the Scavaig River, to an isolated spot overlooking Loch Coruisk. It was a remote area, and they had not expected to see anyone else. However, they were surprised to see a young, slender man walking aimlessly on the rocky slopes next to the loch.

They asked him; "Hello. Are you lost?".

"Yes", came the reply.

"What's your name?", the pair enquired.

"I'm sorry, I don't know", came the answer.

A further conversation revealed that the man was quite genuine. He had no idea who he was, what he was doing on Skye, or how he had got there. The yachtsmen radioed Mallaig for assistance and took the enigmatic stranger on board with them.

Once back in Mallaig, Inspector MacDonald, from Fort William police station, questioned the man. The stranger could not shed any light on how he had reached the Isle of Skye, his name, what his occupation was, or how long he had been on the island. Inspector

MacDonald had the man transferred to hospital in Fort William, for observation, and decided to make some enquiries. The inspector requested information on all missing persons reported to the authorities in the previous few weeks. This was a far more laborious process in 1938 than it is today. Meanwhile, the man was attended to at the recently extended Belford Hospital in Fort William. Despite many questions and tests, the man was unable to shed any light on how he had ended up by the side of a remote loch on Skye. A newspaper appeal for witnesses yielded two possible sightings of the unknown man in Mallaig on 25th and 30th July, and one at the Morar Highland Games on August 1st. Meanwhile the police were able to narrow down their trawl through the register of people reported by members of the public. The man was fairly young, probably 30 or under. He had an English accent and seemed to be a Londoner. With this in mind, Inspector MacDonald was able to narrow his search to the South East of England. On the 9th August he received details from Paddington police station in London, of a young man reported missing three weeks previously. The report included a photograph of the missing man. Armed with the black and white image, Inspector MacDonald visited the man in hospital during the afternoon.

"Have you heard the name Ralph Waldo Vernon?", the inspector inquired.

The man sat up and grabbed the police officer's arm, "Yes! That's me!"

Mr Ralph Waldo Vernon was a 28-year-old clerk with a small manufacturing company in Paddington. He lived at 14 Portobello Road, in Notting Hill, London. At the beginning of January 1938 he had been involved in a serious motoring accident during which he had suffered some head injuries. After a long period of rehabilitation Vernon was thought to have recovered. However, a further slight accident in June, in which he may have received a further knock to the head, was thought to have exacerbated his injuries.

Despite fully recovering physically and being returned to his family in London, Vernon was never able to account for the missing three weeks. Even though he had been reported missing by his family, he had somehow managed to travel from Paddington to Mallaig (a distance of 555 miles) without any reported sightings, nor any memory of how he had travelled there. Despite having been in the Mallaig area for a least a week, only three sightings were made. Ralph Vernon was also not able to recall how he reached the Island of Skye or how he had ended up wandering aimlessly on the banks of Loch Coruisk. Exactly what did happen during those three weeks, and what mysteriously drew him to the west of Scotland, has always remained a mystery.

The summer of 1946 was a pleasant one on the West coast of Scotland. George Orwell had rented a house on Jura, in order to write his dystopian novel *Nineteen Eighty-Four*. He was to spend 18 months there. Scotland had recently beaten England 1 – 0 in the Victory

International at Hampden Park, in front of more than 139,000 people. Meanwhile the motor boat *Betty* and the fishing trawler *Fountain* were taking advantage of the calm seas and both left the harbour at Stornoway at midday on Saturday 17th August. *Betty* arrived safely at Mallaig at 2am on Sunday morning. The *Fountain* did not. There was immediate fear for the nine-man crew, which included popular skipper Angus Nicolson and his two sons. An immediate search of the area was made by the fishing cruiser *Longa,* in the neighbourhood of Kebock Head, a rocky and isolated headland on the east coast of Lewis, where a boat had been sighted. There was no sign of the missing trawler, however, and it was thought that the craft sighted earlier may have been a southward bound vessel. Later on that day, the coastguard received a report that a boat had been spotted passing the lighthouse on South Rona Island at approximately 7pm on the previous evening. However, they were unable to confirm the

vessel. The last confirmed sighting of the *Fountain* was made at 2.30pm on Saturday, by the *Ocean Searcher*, who spotted the missing trawler near the Shiant Islands, off Lewis in the Outer Hebrides. Coastguard stations along the north west coast began an extensive quest and the RAF were asked to assist with an aerial search.

It was thought the vessel may have sought shelter in one of the inland lochs, or perhaps drifted with engine trouble. The mystery deepened as no further sightings were made and the search was called off until morning light.

On the following morning, as the RAF were about to commence operations, the coastguard at Mallaig received a telephone call. It was Angus Nicolson, the captain of the *Fountain*.

"We're okay!", blurted out the captain, "we had engine trouble and decided to dump the catch and land at Glenfield."

It was his first opportunity to call. Much to the relief of all the families concerned, everyone was safe. The crew of the *Fountain* were lucky on this occasion. But with more than 100 charted shipwrecks off the west coast of Scotland (and hundreds more unaccounted for) the risks are very real, with fishermen taking their lives in their own hands every day.

One mystery that was not resolved so easily, sadly, took place in August 1970. Mallaig lobster fisherman Cyril Simpson, aged 21, was at sea just off the coast of

Mallaig, close to the mouth of Loch Nevis. He spotted a woman's body floating in the water. The body, he thought, had been in the water no more than 24 hours and was wearing a yellow life jacket, a black coat and skirt. He noticed that the woman was wearing gold jewellery and rings and appeared to be about 30 - 40 years of age. Simpson tried to drag the body aboard but each time his dinghy nearly capsized. Worried that he would be dragged into the cold, dark water himself he tied some rope to the body – to act as a marker – and rowed back to shore to inform the police and coastguard. When the sun rose, the police began the search of the area pointed out by Simpson, but no body could be located. Either the current had swept it seaward or the weight of the rope had dragged the unfortunate woman to the loch floor.

The police feared that a boat or canoe may have foundered nearby and launched an appeal to secretaries of yachting and sailing clubs. However, no one came forward with the name of a missing vessel. The mystery deepened the following day when a white van was reported to police. It appeared to have been abandoned on the outskirts of Mallaig. Witnesses reported that the van had been seen with a canoe on its roof a few days previously.

Despite extensive efforts the woman's body was never identified.

THE INVERLAIR CRASH

The dark and windy roads of Lochaber were, and can still be, a dangerous place. Although it is not always criminals that we need to look out for. Sometimes it can be criminally bad legislation. If any of the stories in this book highlight the differences between life a century ago and now, this one surely does.

As mentioned in the earlier chapter on life and hardship in the Monessie Camp, tragedy can strike anywhere, and at any time. The workers employed at the Lochaber Hydro Power Scheme suffered greatly from a lack of modern health and safety legislation while working. The events of 15th August 1925 show that even their recreation time could be marred by disaster.

After a gruelling week of work, the construction workers at Fersit Camp in Tulloch, near Inverlair, were looking forward to an evening drink at the Roy Bridge Hotel. Twelve men wanted to make the eight-mile journey that Saturday night from the workers' huts into Roy Bridge. One of the men, James

Simpson, was persuaded to drive. He seemed to be the most qualified driver among the group, having approximately nine years' experience behind the wheel. The group decided to borrow one of the motor lorries belonging to the main contractor, Messrs Balfour Beatty, for the journey. The unauthorised use of the company's vehicles was strictly forbidden. However it appeared that the foreman had gone home for the weekend and the lorry had been left unattended. In 1925 there was no formal driving test for either motor cars or heavy goods vehicles. It would be another decade before these were introduced to Scotland's roads. The 'designated driver' was very often the man who was either the most experienced, or the man felt by the group to be best able to 'hold his drink'.

When the men departed Fersit Camp in the open backed truck it was still daylight, the end of a pleasant summer's day. Nine men sat on the floor of the flatbed back of the truck, their legs dangling over the side, the remaining three men sat in the driver's cab. The bumps and twists of the narrow track from the camp, past the River Treig, jolted the men back and forward. Even those in the cab were uncomfortable on the wooden seats, under the thin wooden canopy.

The men, who all hailed from the Stirling area, knew each other well. Two were father and son, William and John Johnstone. and they passed a pleasant evening in Roy Bridge. James Simpson, the driver, downed three pints of beer and a whisky or two during the evening.

At a quarter to nine the men in the party climbed back aboard the lorry and set off for the camp at Fersit. It was darker now and vehicle headlights were much less effective than they are today. The road (now the A86) was narrower in 1925 than it is today and cat's eyes, to help guide the night-time motorist, were not patented for another 10 years (when inventor Percy Shaw was narrowly able to avoid crashing at a sharp bend in the road, thanks to his car's headlights reflecting in the eyes of a cat perched on a roadside fence).

Twice during the journey back to their camp the men sitting in the back were alarmed when their vehicle swerved for a moment, leaving the road and skidding along the grass verge. Charlie Harper and John Johnstone remembered a thud and a jolt as the truck veered from left to right. They glanced at each other but remembered that James Simpson seemed perfectly capable of driving when they had departed the hotel at Roy Bridge. Their truck turned right, off the main road and onto the narrow twisting track leading up to the Fersit camp. Rough stone chippings covered the track and, at its nearest points to the River Treig, there was barely an inch or two's gap between the edge of the track and the steep embankment dropping down to the river.

The track was windy and narrow, requiring skill and nerve even during daylight. It was now quite dark. Suddenly, without warning, at a particularly sharp and dangerous bend in the road, the lorry's wheels turned just too late. In a split second the weight and momentum of the vehicle sent it careering off the track and down the steep, 30-feet precipice and into the River Treig below. The sudden and sharp drop in the dark of the night must have been terrifying. Instantly, as the lorry tumbled out of control down the incline it flipped and somersaulted three times, throwing the nine men positioned in the open back of the vehicle completely free. They were thrown and catapulted ahead of the lorry and crashed into the water below. Instantly, on hitting the water, they turned to see the vehicle hurtling down the bank towards them.

Remarkably, the truck landed on its wheels and seven of the men were lucky enough to be protected from certain death by the narrow clearance between the underside of the truck and the riverbed. They escaped with cuts and bruises. Two men were not so lucky. William Johnstone, aged 53, and Donald Orr, aged 25, were crushed to death. The three men in the cab were tossed from floor to ceiling as the truck careered down the embankment but, although concussed and battered, managed to escape.

The men thrown clear (of course there were no seatbelts then), although dazed and injured, managed to climb and scramble up the bank and went to fetch help. Peter Gow was lucky on this occasion. Two weeks earlier he had been involved in another road accident. This time, despite having lost the use of one arm in the previous accident, he managed to pull himself to safety. John O'Hara, Harry Fussler, William Stewart and Charlie Harper all went to fetch help. John Johnstone stayed and tried to locate his father William. Sadly, his father was one of the two men killed.

Dr McIver, from Fort William – who happened to be nearby – was first on the scene, shortly followed by Dr McIntosh, the resident medical officer for the contractors. They treated the men as best they could, until further help arrived.

The Procurator-Fiscal and Inspector of Police arrived in the morning light to investigate the accident. The decision was made to place the driver James Simpson under arrest and he was removed to Fort William Police Station. Following an investigation lasting several weeks he was charged with culpable homicide:

James Simpson, you did on the night of 15th August 1925, while in a state of intoxication, drive a motor lorry, which contained about a dozen men, in a culpable and reckless manner, whereby it was upset and precipitated over a wall, causing the death of William Johnstone and Donald Orr, and that you did kill them outright.

The case against James Simpson was heard at Fort William Courthouse on 20th October 1925. Sheriff-Substitute Steedman oversaw proceedings. One by one the remaining men recounted the events of the 15th August to the court. They were questioned by the Crown and asked to recall how much James Simpson had drunk on that evening and whether, in their opinion, he was capable of driving the motor lorry home. None of the men could be exactly sure of how much alcohol had been consumed (they had all indulged too) but it was estimated that Simpson had drunk 'three pints of beer and one or two whiskies'. Simpson himself, speaking as the only defence witness, stated that he had consumed three pints of beer and nothing else.

All the men thought he was capable of driving the vehicle back to the camp.

After summing up, the jury were excused, returning with a unanimous verdict of 'Not Guilty'. James Simpson was released. Drink-driving, as we know it today, did not became an offence until the 1960s, with no actual blood alcohol limit introduced until January 1966. The breathalyser test did not appear on Scotland's roads until 1967. Whilst a driver could still be prosecuted in the 1920s if it was felt he had driven in a 'reckless manner', the attitude in society was very much the one demonstrated in this case. If a person said they were capable of driving, that seemed to satisfy the majority. In incidents such as the one above, a fine of 40 shillings was the usual punishment.

The Road Traffic Act of 1930 did go some way to tightening the law, although there was still no measurable drink driving limit. Sadly, however, it came too late for William Johnstone and Donald Orr.

THE EXPERT SWORDSMAN

Donald McBane was a soldier, pimp, thief, gambler and duellist. He was also a natural genius with the smallsword (the lighter successor to the rapier) and lived a life so colourful and dangerous it is surprising he managed to survive long enough to write his autobiography.

McBane was born in 1664 in Inverness, where his family kept a farm and public house. He was originally apprenticed to a tobacco-spinner (tobacconist). However he soon tired of this when the meals he was served, as part of his pay, were reduced in size. He immediately decided to leave and enlist in the Royalist Army. It was 1687, and McBane was 23 years of age. He did not have to wait long before he found himself in the thick of the action. In August of the following year he fought for the Clan Mackintosh against the Keppoch MacDonalds, in what became known as the Battle of Mulroy (Maol Ruadh) in Lochaber. It had been agreed that the Clan Mackintosh were to be given government support. Soldiers – including

Donald McBane – were despatched to fight, however they were no match for the MacDonalds of Keppoch (who had been described as 'virtually professional bandits'). McBane would later describe the battle in his autobiography;

The MacDonalds came down the Hill upon us without either shoe, stocking, or bonnet on their head. They broke in upon us with sword, targe (shield) and Lochaber axes. Seeing my Captain sore wounded, and a great many more with heads lying cloven on every side, I was sadly affrighted, never having seen the like before … I took to my heels, and ran thirty miles, before I looked behind me.

The Mackintoshes and McBane's government troops were soundly beaten. If the experience was not frightening enough, within two years he would find himself taking to his heels again to save his own skin. The Battle of Killiecrankie (Blàr Choille Chnagaidh), took place on 27 July 1689 during the first Jacobite rising, between Claverhouse's Jacobite force of Scots and Irish against those of the new Williamite government, under General Hugh MacKay. The Jacobites won a stunning victory and, chased by a Highlander waving a pistol and sword, McBane took to his heels running towards the River Garry, where he jumped 18 feet over the deep water, on to the rocky western bank, at a place now commemorated in the name the 'Soldier's Leap'. He then stole a horse from his unit's own baggage train, and rode away, with a Highlander's bullet whistling past his ear.

By 1690 his regiment were 'camped at Inverlochy in Lochaber, at which time we began to build Fort William.' McBane had begun fencing lessons following an argument with a senior officer who had allegedly stolen his pay packet, and he soon became an expert swordsman. However, his 'Highland blood warmed' in arguments, leading to several duels. After wounding another senior officer, he was obliged to leave one regiment for another, eventually ending up in Ireland for a time where he would later relate in his autobiography tales of fights, duels, and women. He even managed to convince a local girl that they were legally married, despite the priest refusing to go through with the ceremony.

After accidentally falling asleep on a troop ship at Leith - following a few drinks - McBane woke up on his way to Holland and began a career on the continent, starting at the siege of Namur, part of the Nine Years' War against France, during which time he was seriously wounded – not for the last time. Whilst on the continent, McBane set up a fencing school to supplement his army pay. He soon realised that other fencing masters were making even more money by also running gaming tents and brothels. He challenged four of the army's leading fencing masters to duels, fighting and defeating them one after another 'like a rogue D'Artagnan' until he made the last one promise to cut him into his brothel and gambling business.

"With this and my school, I lived very well for that winter", McBane remarked with his characteristic matter-of-factness.

His extraordinary career continued. McBane kept 16 'professors of the sword' and 60 women at his fencing school/brothel, even making enough money to marry again. His wife, a formidable woman, helped in the business by selling beer and 'genever' (gin) to soldiers.

By 1709, she and McBane had at least two children. During the battle of Malplaquet their three-year-old son was left in the safe-keeping of another woman, but when the child-minder heard that her own husband was dead, she rode with the child to the front line, then, as McBane describes in another masterpiece of understatement:

She threw the boy at me; then I was obliged to put him in my habersack [rucksack] ... and as we were inclining to the right, the boy got a shot in the arm, I then got a surgeon and dressed it, I had neither bread nor drink to give him, I got a dram to him from an officer and a leg of a fowl, then he held his peace...

McBane's wife rescued her son the following morning.

McBane continued to live his life in this breathless style, later recounting the 27 times he was wounded (not including the occasion when he was blown up by his own hand grenade), his 16 battles, 15 skirmishes and nearly 100 duels.

He eventually retired, aged 48, and became a Chelsea Pensioner in London and opened an alehouse, although he did briefly return to the army during the 1715 Jacobite risings. In his retirement he took part in various exhibition fights, during which time he fought at the famous 'Beargarden' gladiatorial contests in London, including one fight against 'England's most celebrated gladiator, James Figg'. Figg maintained a record of 270 wins and was considered Britain's top swordsman. Sadly, there is no record of the outcome of their contest.

On the 23rd June 1726 at the Abbey of Holyrood House, Edinburgh, McBane (now aged 63) fought the Irish gladiator, Andrew O'Bryen before a large crowd. He inflicted seven wounds on the Irishman before finally breaking his arm with the fauchion (a short broadsword curved sharply to a point). The *Edinburgh Evening Courant* reported that; "Old Donald McBane, from the north of Scotland, did quite defeat the Irishman, and almost cut him to pieces, and shamefully beat him off the stage, for challenging the whole country". The contest seems to have been enough for McBane however who, shortly afterwards, resolved "never to fight any more but to repent for my former wickedness". He retired to Fort William in the autumn of 1726 and set about writing his autobiography, *The Expert Swordsman's Companion,* which became a best seller and one of the most fascinating autobiographies written in the English language. He died on 12th April 1732, four years after the book's publication.

McBane was believed to have been buried in the Craigs graveyard in Fort William; however his final resting place was assumed to have been lost or destroyed. With no one able to locate his gravestone, the *Fort William Guidebook* of 1881 sadly reported that 'unfortunately it is broken or lost.'

However, in a footnote to Donald McBane's remarkable life, local historian Andrew Wiseman, from the School of Scottish Studies, stumbled across a letter published in the *Inverness Courier* in 1889, detailing the exact position of the famous swordsman's grave:

You'll not know it's there as the name has long since been erased – in part because it was only lightly engraved and in part because we as children used to slide down it... It has a skull and crossbones and is on the east side of the Craigs low down.

This remarkable and poignant monument to a most extraordinary man is still there today for all to see, close to the small gate at the east end of the Craigs graveyard.

SAVED FROM THE PLAGUE

Around the year 1639 a tragic love story took place in Callart on the southern shores of Loch Leven.

Mary Cameron was the daughter of Ewan Cameron, laird of Callart, and was very popular among the poorer people of the local community. She had endeared herself to those less fortunate with many acts of kindness, mercy and generosity. Mary frequently gave away clothing and money to those in need. However, her behaviour displeased her father greatly, who thought that Mary should not fraternise with the peasantry.

One day in the summer of 1639 news reached the area that a Spanish trading ship would be arriving at Ballachulish, laden with luxury goods for sale. The laird decided he would take his family to view the wares for sale, which included rich fabrics, clothing, fine cottons, silks and satins for ladies' dresses. The laird, his wife and all his children were allowed to visit the ship, with the exception of Mary (who had infuriated her father by giving half of her wardrobe away to a poor woman in the district). Mary was locked in an upstairs room of Callart House and the party left without her. In the course of time her family returned and Mary could hear, from the confines of her room, the sounds of animated talking and laughing as her family discussed their purchases. Eventually the talking subsided and the house fell still. Mary retired to bed.

In the morning the house was still and quiet. Mary tried the door but it was still locked. She called out and banged her hand on the wooden frame. Still there was no answer. Finally, after a considerable wait, Mary managed to force the door of her room open. She called out, but no one answered. Hurriedly she searched the house, firstly opening the door to her parent's chamber. Their bodies lay side-by-side, blackened and lifeless. As Mary looked in the other bedrooms she discovered the bodies of her five brothers and sister, motionless and dead, their skin blackened and their faces contorted in pain. Mary, although completely distraught, knew at once from the evidence before her, that her family had succumbed to the plague. The plague (also known as the Black Death or Bubonic Plague) had infected many parts of the country and, despite its rural setting and smaller population, Lochaber was not immune. Black Death was much feared among the population, and Mary had no doubt heard stories of the disease and recognised the tell-tale signs. Sufferers could succumb to any, or all, of the symptoms. Fever and chills. Extreme weakness. Abdominal pain, diarrhoea and vomiting. Bleeding from your mouth, nose or rectum, or even from under your skin. Finally, shock and a blackening of the skin tissue (gangrene) in your extremities, most commonly your fingers, toes and nose.

There had been several outbreaks, even as far afield as the Scottish Islands. The disease seemed to have reached ports and docks around Scotland by ship and the Privy Council had banned the arrival of any boat into Scottish ports from either London or the Netherlands. In other cases, action was taken to quarantine ships and crew, or even burn suspected vessels. Unknown to the people of Ballachulish, the Spanish ship had already called at an infected city and had been blacklisted from several future ports of call.

Mary knew she must avoid contact with the bodies and hurriedly gathered some food into her arms and returned to her bedroom, shutting the door behind herself. As Mary pondered what to do, she heard voices from below her window. She recognised one of the men as Donald Cameron from Ballachulish, whose family Mary had recently befriended and helped. She called down from the window, pleading for his help. Donald informed Mary that the story of the plague was already known and his party had been sent to burn down the house, with everything and everybody inside it. However, as some small return for Mary's kindness towards his family, Donald Cameron agreed to take a message to Mary's lover Patrick, or Diarmid, Campbell of Loch Awe and delay the torching of the house until the following evening. In the meantime, the house was boarded up with Mary still inside.

On receiving the news, Diarmid immediately gathered eight of his best men and the group set sail for Callart House, via Loch Etive and Loch Linnhe, arriving under cover of darkness. One version of the story tells us that they lowered a rope, tied to a chimney, and rescued Mary. Another that they propped a ladder against the wall. As soon as Mary was free, Diarmid told her to wash herself in the nearby burn and destroy her clothes. He wrapped her in a blanket he had brought with him and they escaped to Loch Awe by boat. Within moments of their departure, the house was ablaze. Mary had dodged death by a matter of minutes.

On their arrival at Loch Awe, news of the plague had already reached Diarmid's father. He addressed the young couple from an upstairs window, forbidding them from entering the house. Diarmid and Mary were told that they must live in isolation for a month before they would be allowed in the family home. He also informed the couple they could not live alone together until they were married. He shouted the legal words of the marriage ceremony from the upstairs window, the couple gave the appropriate responses, and he solemnly declared them married! The newlyweds were then directed to a remote cottage in the Pass of Awe, where they lived for a month in peaceful isolation.

When their time had passed, the couple returned to the ancestral home and celebrated their marriage. It appears that they had a son, John, not long afterwards. Diarmid was proud of Mary's beauty and named her Mary the Lily of Callart, or the Fair Maid of Callart. Sadly, it appears that Diarmid died not long afterwards, in 1645 at the Battle of Inverlochy. Their son John, an uncanny likeness of his father, reminded Mary so intensely of her late husband, her sorrow was recorded in a Gaelic verse, known as Mary's Lament:

You took me from the house of pestilence

Where died my father and my mother,

My sister and my five brothers.

And; There are deer on the little isle of the Yews

And trout in the pool of the marsh

And though there are, what use are they to me,

And my beloved Patrick, he lies in the vault of the church.

Mary lived a long life. However, as her family were lost to the Black Death and her childhood home razed to the ground, she never returned to Callart. Eventually in the 1790s another house was built there. The remains of the original dwelling can still be seen in the grounds.

LOST GOLD

To the north of Fort William, west of the Great Glen, lies Loch Arkaig (Gaelic: Loch Airceig), a mysterious expanse of water 12 miles in length and up to 300 feet in depth. It is thought that somewhere on the shores or hillsides surrounding the loch is buried a treasure so important that its historical worth cannot be measured. Its monetary value can be however - and has been estimated to be somewhere in the region of £10 million today.

When Bonnie Prince Charlie (Prince Charles Edward Stuart) landed on Scottish shores at Loch nan Uamh, on the West coast in 1745, to raise the Jacobite banner and begin the rebellion, he promised his supporters that he had been assured the support of the French and Spanish armies in the fight against the British. In fact, neither the French or the Spanish governments ever intended to support him militarily but did offer financial support in the form of money and supplies.

Spain pledged some 400,000 Louis d'Or gold coins per month to help the Jacobite cause. Minted in 1745 by Louis XV of France each coin was 24 carats. Due to the excellent minting techniques (which were almost impossible to forge), their quality and fineness, the coins could be used as international trading currency. Transporting this money to the rebel army was a difficult and hazardous operation. The first instalment (sent via Charles's brother Henry who was resident in France at the time) was dispatched in 1745. This was followed, on 25 March 1746, by a French ship especially re-named *Le Prince Charles*, formerly the *HMS Hazard*, which carried £13,000 in gold, arms and other supplies to Inverness for the Jacobite leader Bonnie Prince Charlie. Unfortunately for the Prince, the ship was forced into the Kyle of Tongue while being pursued by the British frigate *HMS Sheerness*. During the night the crew and soldiers disembarked carrying the money. However the following morning Captain George Mackay, son of the chief of the Clan Mackay, a supporter of the British government and King George II, confronted them at a place named Drum Nan Coup. In a short fight called the Skirmish of Tongue, Mackay captured the men and the money.

Despite the setback, and true to their word, the Spanish again tried to send financial support to Bonnie Prince Charlie and his Jacobite followers. On 30th April 1746 seven casks of gold coins, containing 1,200,000 French and Spanish gold coins, were landed on the West coast of Scotland by two French frigates, the *Bellona* and *Mars*. The crew on board the ships had not yet heard of the recent defeat of Bonnie Prince Charlie at the Battle of Culloden and were rushing to help the Jacobites. As the French ships landed, they were spotted by British navy warships and they hastily unloaded their cargo so they could head out to confront the incoming warships in open water. After some intense fighting, the French seemingly damaged one of the British warships and were able to make their escape back to France, leaving the precious cargo of gold coins behind.

As the Jacobite cause was by then lost, with the army scattered across the Highlands and Prince Charles and his loyal lieutenants in hiding, it was decided that the money should be used to assist the Jacobite clansmen, who by this time were being subjected to the brutalities of the Duke of Cumberland's redcoat army, and to help facilitate the escape to France of wanted Jacobite soldiers and supporters.

Six caskets (one having already been stolen by McDonald of Barrisdale's men) were carried inland for 20 miles to Loch Arkaig and temporarily hidden. Their secret was entrusted to Murray of Broughton, one of the Jacobite fugitives. Murray then began the distribution of the gold coins to clan chiefs. Meanwhile the Duke of Cumberland ordered a march into Lochaber of 1,700 government troops, under the Earl of Loudon, to quell any attempt at an uprising. Murray of Broughton was apprehended by the British government (and turned state's evidence in exchange for his life). This forced the remaining Jacobite leaders to entrust the treasure, first to Lochiel, the chief of Clan Cameron, and then to Euan Macpherson of Cluny, head of Clan Macpherson. MacPherson spent many years hiding in a cave at Ben Alder, which came to be known as 'Cluny's Cage'. At this stage, it seems, Cluny still maintained control of what was left of the Jacobite money.

Bonnie Prince Charles finally escaped Scotland in the French frigate *L'Heureux* and arrived back in France, via the Isle of Skye, in September 1746. However, the fate of the treasure is not quite so clear. MacPherson of Cluny is believed to have retained control of it, and during his long years as a fugitive was at the centre of various futile plots to finance another Jacobite uprising. Indeed, he remained in hiding in his Highland 'cage' for the next eight years (which formed the basis for part of Robert Louis Stevenson's novel *Kidnapped*). Meanwhile, a cash-strapped Prince Charles was desperately hoping for the treasure to be returned to him in France. At least some of it did find its way back to France, paying for the minting of a campaign medal in 1750. However, the majority of the gold was never recovered. Charles, years later, accused Cluny, who was certainly never able to fully account for the whereabouts of all of the gold coins, of embezzlement.

Indeed, as is usual with such a vast fortune, the gold became a source of discord, mistrust and grievance among the surviving Jacobites.

It is probable that Doctor Archibald Cameron (Lochiel's brother, who was acting as secretary to the Prince) made an early return to Scotland in 1749 in pursuit of the treasure, and did successfully return some of the gold coins to Prince Charles, which may account for his being able to finance the minting of campaign medals. Dr Cameron, on his return to France in 1750, produced a detailed memorandum regarding the movement of the gold coins. This record, along with Cluny's account outlining the distribution of the monies, is contained in the *Stuart Papers*. Some of the pages and entries are missing, lost over time. However the accounts do show a substantial amount of money still missing, increasing the probability that a large number of coins may still be hidden somewhere. The details are listed over in abbreviated form:

An account of 35,000 Louis d'Ors sent from France and landed on the West of Scotland at the beginning of May 1746 by order of Sir Thomas Sheridan and Mr Murray Secretary to His Royal Highness.

		<u>35,000</u>
Stolen at the time of landing by a fellow who went abroad		800
Given to different corps of the army for arrears due some months before, and towards charges to bring their men to a rendezvous against a day appointed		4,200
Carried south by Mr Murray and lodged at Edinburgh		3,000
Brought abroad by HR.Highness in Sept 1746		3,000
Clunie's Acct. of the (remaining) 24,000 Louis	24,000	
Different setts of people as per particular directions in writing		750
In Angus Cameron hands		3,000
To J Cameron of Fassiefern to pay the stipens of Lochiel's estate		350
On account for the houses of several whose houses were burned and their cattle carried away		500
To Fassiefern for his expenses and in order to enable him to label the claims upon Locheil's estate		100
To Major Kennedy		6,000
Exhausted in support of myself, servants, secretaries, and for the subsistence of my family and children f or the space of four years		1,200
Part of the money that was lost and never recovered		481
		<u>11,619</u>

Both Dr Cameron's account, and that of Cluny, differ and there were further claims and counterclaims, however both versions show a substantial amount of money unaccounted for. It should also be added that Major Kennedy was accused of gambling away his share!

In 1753, Doctor Archibald Cameron was sent back to Scotland on a covert mission, not only to secure the remaining treasure, but help orchestrate an assassination plot to murder King George II. However, whilst staying secretly at Brenachyle by Loch Katrine, he was betrayed (apparently by the notorious 'Pickle', a government spy) and arrested. He was charged under the Act of Attainder for his part in the 1745 uprising. The act, passed in 1702, enabled the government to declare a person guilty of a crime, then carry out punishment, without a trial. Archibald Cameron was sentenced to death and, on 7th June 1753, was drawn on a sledge to Tyburn in London where his punishment was carried out. It is said he died with great courage and resolution. After he had been hung, his entrails and heart were thrown on to an open fire. He was 45 years old and the last man to die for the Jacobite cause.

Following Dr Cameron's arrest and execution in 1753, the trail of the lost treasure goes cold. Many believed the gold was still buried, somewhere close to Loch Arkaig. One version tells of the treasure being placed in a deep hole close to the loch. Some believe it may have been moved elsewhere. It was certainly never recovered by the British government.

Tantalising clues still remain, however.

Walter Scott, the novelist, and the historian Andrew Lang both researched the *Stuarts Papers* (now in the possession of the Queen). These reveal a host of claims and accusations between the exiled Jacobites and Clan chiefs, as to the fate of the treasure. The papers also include a detailed account, drawn up by Archibald Cameron in around 1750 before he returned to Scotland, detailing Cluny's inability to account for the whereabouts of all the gold coins.

The respected historian William D Chambers, writing approximately 100 years after the treasure was lost, recorded a surprisingly detailed account of a gathering of men at Kinlocharkaig, an isolated spot at the west end of Loch Arkaig, where several burns from the River Pean flow into the loch:

the time fixed for the rendezvous was altered to a week later, during which interval 15,000 of the Louis d'Ors were secretly buried in the wood on the south side of Loch Arkaig, about a mile and a half from the head of the loch, by Doctor Cameron, in the presence of Sir Stuart Thriepland, Major Kennedy, and Mr. Alexander MacLeod Divided into three parcels of 5,000 Louis d'Ors each, two of which were buried in the ground and (the third placed under a rock in a small rivulet).

Despite this enticing and detailed clue, no one has yet been able to locate the lost gold. The River Pean flows between Lochan Leum an t-sagairt and Loch Arkaig for about eight miles. Within a mile and a half of the head of Loch Arkaig there are six burns that flow into the River Pean on the south side. Despite several searches in recent years no one has yet managed to uncover the treasure.

For a time, it was also believed that Dr Cameron and Alexander MacLeod hid some of the money at Achnacarry Castle but hastily removed it on hearing that government troops intended to search there. It was recorded that they then hid the gold 'near the foot of Loch Arkaig.'

Perhaps, however, MacPherson of Cluny removed the treasure from its hiding place close to the loch and concealed it in his mountainside cage (Cluny's Cage), somewhere on Ben Alder. Modern Ordnance Survey maps of Ben Alder mark a spot known as *'Prince Charlie's Cave'*, however nobody has ever found a cave at this remote location. Margaret Elphinstone, a lecturer in English studies at Strathclyde University, has offered a solution to this mystery. She concluded that there never was a cave as marked on maps. She believes early mapmakers merely confused the word 'cage' for 'cave', claiming that early maps actually marked the location of 'Cluny's Cage' which could have been the elaborately constructed refuge of Cluny of Clan Macpherson. Legend tells us that his cage was said to have been located somewhere on the southern slopes of Ben Alder facing the north western shore of Loch Ericht. A tantalising clue was written in a journal by Donald MacPherson, which became part of a folio of documents collated by Bishop Robert Forbes between 1747 – 1775:

Twas situated in the face of a very rough high rocky mountain called Letternilichk, which is still a part of Ben Alder, full of great stones and crevices and some scattered wood interspersed. The habitation called the Cage in the face of that mountain was within a small thick bush of wood.

To offer hope to those who believe the gold may still be unclaimed, is a note of a conversation between Donald MacPherson and the Prince, also recorded in the same folio of documents. In a moment of optimism, the Prince exclaimed; "It is remarkable that my enemies have not discovered one farthing of my money".

Further clues to support this theory can also be found among the pages of Robert Louis Stevenson's *Kidnapped*. Margaret Elphinstone (who knew that Stevenson, when writing *Kidnapped*, borrowed heavily from Cluny's younger brother's description of the 'Cage'), combed the isolated area and found rocks that formed a natural fireplace, exactly matching Stevenson's description of the back of the cage in his novel. It is also well known that Bonnie Prince Charlie spent some time hiding with Cluny, at his cave, before eventually fleeing to France. Would it not make sense, then, that at least some of the gold could have been hidden here? Perhaps, yet considering that the location is marked on Ordnance Survey maps, it seems too obvious a place to search for the treasure now.

There is another contradictory location for 'Cluny's Cage' however, which may not have yet been found or explored. Perhaps this holds the key to the secret of the lost Jacobite gold. After all, as Robert Louis Stevenson explained in *Kidnapped* that Cluny's Cage "was but one of Cluny's hiding-places; he had caves, besides, and underground chambers in several parts of his country". The novel also contains a detailed description of the hiding place, in which the terrain around the exterior is described;

As we came at last to the foot of an exceeding steep wood, which scrambled up a craggy hillside, and was crowned by a naked precipice…Quite at the top, and just before the rocky face of the cliff sprang above the foliage.

Note the historical description of a rocky cliff face above the hide-out. This site was deliberately chosen as the dark colour of the cliff face would disguise the smoke from their fires. There are no cliffs above the 'Prince Charles Cave' marked on Ordnance Survey maps. In any event, the track just below the site was so close that soldiers on patrol would smell the smoke. However, there is a location on the opposite side of Loch Ericht that perfectly matches the description and has yet to be properly explored. Opposite Alder Bay sits a huge crag affording a sentry an excellent view of the loch. Above it sit gigantic and imposing slabs of rock sweeping down from the hill top. They seem to match exactly the colour and type of rock face capable of camouflaging smoke rising from the Cage. Modern maps name this destination as 'Creag na h-Iolaire' (the Crag of the Eagle) and it seems to offer another possible site for the burial of Bonnie Prince Charlie's lost gold. The National Library of Scotland in Edinburgh possesses a map of the west bank of Loch Ericht, completed by James Stobie in 1783. At a spot opposite Alder Bay the map is clearly marked: ''Place where CS hid himself 1746'. The map, of course, was completed less than 40 years after the treasure was lost and was no doubt compiled with the assistance of those for whom the event was in living memory. Further evidence that marks the west bank of Loch Ericht as the location of Bonnie Prince Charlie's cave can be found in a little known book written in 1796 by an English lady during her Highland tour. The Honourable Sarah Murray was conveyed to the spot by a local boatman and described it clearly in her book, *A Companion and Useful Guide to the Beauties of Scotland*:

The lake looks like a broad river, with immense, and most of them bare craggy mountains, rising perpendicularly from it; except here and there alpine wood creeping up their sides, till the shivering stones debar vegetation. On the east bank of this lake, at the south end of it where I embarked, is a prodigiously high, rough, bare mountain, in the hollows of which, as I have before mentioned, poor Charles Stuart concealed himself.

She continues by mentioning just how remote – and therefore suitable – a hiding place the land around Loch Ericht was for Prince Charles:

I think there cannot, in nature, be a more forlorn or desolate place than that about Loch Ericht.

In the modern era no one has come forward claiming to have found the treasure. Perhaps, in the months and years following its burial, one of those with inside knowledge helped themselves to a share of the gold. Those who mysteriously came into sudden, and unexplained, wealth were often suggested to have acquired 'Sporrain ghobhlach do dh' or a Phrionnsa' (forked purses of the Prince's gold).

However, there are three more clues which suggest more strongly that the lost gold remains buried somewhere on the shores of Loch Arkaig.

Firstly, the Clan Cameron archives record that before Archibald Cameron was arrested, he and Alexander MacMillan of Glenpeanmore:

Hid the Prince's gold at the Callich burn while Hanoverian troops were hot on their heels coming from Murlaggan private burial-ground where they hid it for a time among loose soil from a newly opened grave.

Murlaggan is an extremely remote hamlet on the north shore of Loch Arkaig, where several burns flow into the loch. Could the previous description from William Chambers have been confused, and the lost gold is actually buried on the north, and not the south side, of the loch? There are several burns located nearby, any of which could feasibly be the hiding place of the treasure. The Clan MacMillan of Murlaggan were also trusted friends of Dr Archibald Cameron and loyal to Bonnie Prince Charlie.

The next clue that lends creditibility to Loch Arkaig being the lost location of the Jacobite gold, was the chance discovery in the 1850s of a leather bag of French and Spanish gold coins found close to Loch Arkaig. The find was only a small one, however, and despite a huge search, no more could be located.

Finally, and perhaps most intriguingly of all was the recent unearthing of a letter which recorded the deathbed confession of one Neill Iain Ruairi. The letter (supposedly written on 6th October 1746) was discovered, quite by accident, tucked into the pages of an old book in a bric-a-brac shop in Winchester, Hampshire.

In the letter Ruairi claimed that he was riding his horse on the footpath passing Loch Arkaig as the treasure was being buried. Wondering what was happening, he carefully concealed himself and observed the clansmen as they buried the gold. As soon as they had left, he quickly helped himself to a bag of coins. However, he heard voices and quickly snatching the bag, he headed to Arisaig, burying the loot along the way, at Camus an talhmuinn, Arisaig.

Unfortunately, not long after hiding his ill-gotten gains he fell from his horse and was badly injured. On his death bed he gave directions to his buried gold stating; *'it was buried near Arisaig under a black stone with a tree root springing from it.'* The letter surfaced again on 17th June 1911 when a doctor in the Arisaig area, Alexander Campbell, found it in an old chest in a house at Kylesmorar. He apparently searched extensively for the gold but found nothing other than

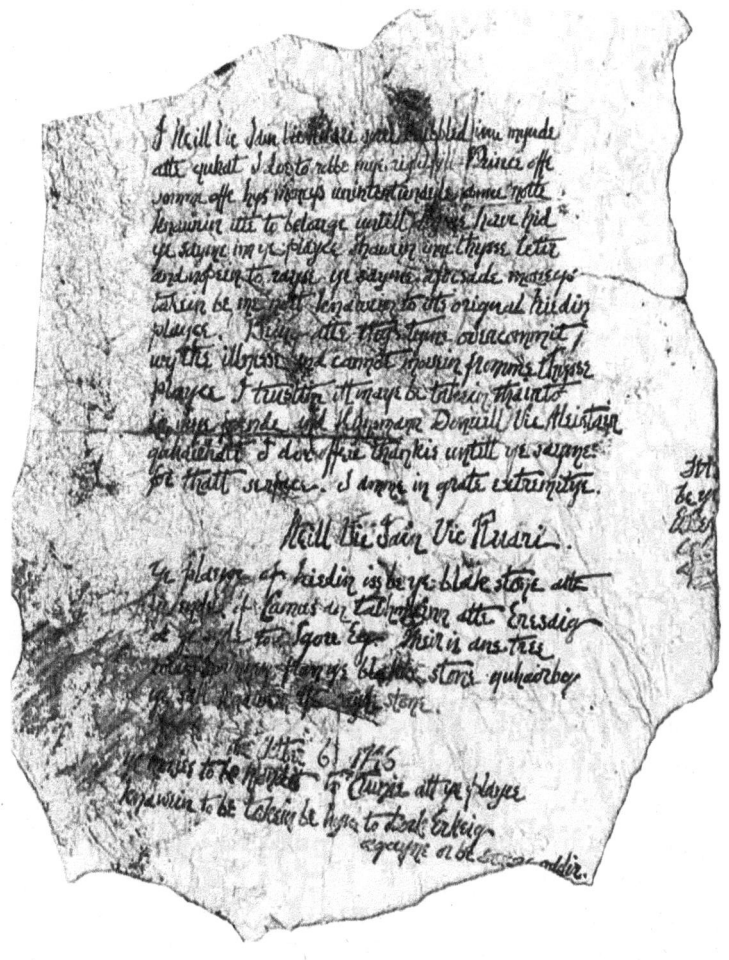

an old (and empty) leather purse. The letter again went missing until it resurfaced again in 2003 in the Winchester secondhand shop. The letter is now kept at the West Highland Museum in Fort William. In 2007 the BBC *History Detectives* series, presented by Neil Oliver, declared the letter to be a fake. However, the letter does contain some very detailed information and authentic period detail. The letter did also lead Dr Alexander Campbell to the empty leather coin purse. If it is a fake, there seems to be no logical reason for it.

In the intervening years many have tried to locate the lost gold of the Jacobites. Anyone is welcome to try. But a word of warning first – not only is the terrain remote and uncompromising but the potential geographical area is huge too. Attempts, ranging from groups of friends with rudimentary metal detectors to well-funded expeditions organised by the BBC, *National Geographic* magazine and *The Sun* newspaper, have all failed.

Expert opinion can offer some advice and comfort though. The hiding place for the gold is likely to be somewhere extremely safe and secure. It is unlikely to be right at the water's edge or underneath a burn. This would leave it too susceptible to changes in the water level, storms or flooding. It is far more likely to be in a cave or hollow, hidden and protected from the vagaries of the Scottish weather. It is also probable that the fleeing Jacobites would have hidden other items of value close by too. A place secure enough to hide hundreds of gold coins would also be a highly suitable place to hide weapons, ammunition and supplies – such as the Jacobite cannon, found close to Loch Arkaig, in the River Loy, as recently as July 2019. Discover evidence of one, and you might well discover evidence of the other. It is also possible, if the gold really was hidden, then in all likelihood, it is still there. Any discovery of this nature and magnitude, even if the discoverer had attempted to hide it, could not have been kept secret. Rumours and speculation would have almost certainly spread.

Lastly, the existing single-track road that skirts the north side of Loch Arkaig is slightly more elevated on the hillside than the original road used by the Jacobites in the 1750s. The previous track was liable to flooding. If the treasure is buried on the north side of the loch, but was hidden adjacent to the original road, it may well be much closer to the waterline than was previously thought. Due to changes in the level of the loch over the past two hundred years, perhaps it is even underwater now?

Wherever the lost gold of the Jacobites is buried, surely one day Loch Arkaig will give up the secret it has guarded so jealously for more than 250 years, and Scotland will be gifted with the most important and valuable archaeological find in its history.

ACKNOWLEDGEMENTS AND REFERENCES

This book would not have been possible without the continued encouragement and help of Kevin & Jayne Ramage and The Highland Bookshop in Fort William. Thank you for your continuing support. I would also like to express my gratitude to the Sarah-Louise Bamblett; Vanessa Martin; Colleen Barker and Sonja McLachlan from the excellent West Highland Museum; Iain Abernethy and Angus MacDonald for pointing me in some interesting directions; Sally Hughes and the very helpful staff at Fort William Public Library; Lochaber Archive Centre; Mallaig Heritage Centre; *The Lochaber Times*; Rev Richard Baxter from Kilmonivaig Parish Church; *West Word Magazine*; Elaine Dunsmore; Ellen McBride; Chris Robinson; Innerpeffray Library and to all the family and friends that have encouraged my endeavours.

The following sources of information have also been invaluable in either helping to piece together the stories contained in this book, or for kindly supplying their permission for the reproduction of images and text:

Lochaber Archive Centre, West Highland Museum, Fort William Public Library, Highland Archive Centre, Mallaig Heritage Centre, SCRAN, Scotland's People, Ordnance Survey, Visions of Britain, The Royal Society of Edinburgh, Margaret Elphinstone, BBC Scotland, Iain Thornber, National Census Archive, The Gazetteer for Scotland, Caledonian Maritime Heritage Trust, History and Horror Scotland, National Library of Scotland

The British Newspaper Archive and the following newspapers and journals;
The Lochaber Times, West Word Magazine, Oban Times, The Scots Magazine, Office for National Statistics, The Press & Journal, Inverness Courier, Dundee Evening Telegraph, Dundee Courier, The Scotsman, Edinburgh Courant, The Evening Post, Aberdeen Weekly Journal, London Gazette, Scottish Field, National Geographic, The Highland News, Liverpool Echo, Loch Ness Survey, Daily Record, The Sun, The Daily Express, Morvern Parochial Board Minutes, The Sunday Post, The Northern Warder, The Elgin Courier, The People's Journal, The Weekly News, The Aberdeen Herald, The Royal Engineers Journal 1934, Sheffield Daily Telegraph, The Guardian.

Bibliography of published resources used:

Whisky Wars by Malcolm Archibald, *Jacobites* by Jacqueline Riding, *Back in Lochaber* by Stuart MacDonald, *Pre 1855 Gravestone Inscriptions in Lochaber* by Lyn and Roger Tatler, *My Ballachulish Childhood* by Marie Campbell, *Tales of Whisky and Smuggling* by Stuart McHardy, *The Crofter and the Laird* by John McPhee, *The Scottish Clearances* by TM Devine, *The Expert Swordsman's Companion* by Donald McBane, *Kidnapped* by Robert Louis Stevenson, *Romantic Lochaber* by Donald B MacCulloch, *The History of the Highland Clearances* by Alexander MacKenzie, *The Highlands* by Calum I Maclean, *Aluminium in the Scottish Highlands* by British Alcan, *Lochaber in Wartime* by Lochaber Local History Society, *The Highland Hotel* by Michael Wells and Chris Lumb, *The Best of the Highlands* by Douglas Gunn, *Tales of the Morar Highlands* by Alasdair Roberts, *Lochaber in War & Peace* by William T Kilgour, *A Week in Wild Lochaber* by W. Pollock, *Fort William and Nether Lochaber* by Mairi MacDonald, *Mountain Outlaw* by Ian R Mitchell, *Lochiel of the '45* by John Sibbald Gibson, *Trial of Duncan Terig* by Sir Walter Scott, *Twelve Scots Trials* by William Roughead, *The Story of the Fort of Fort William* by Edith MacGregor, *The Journals of William D Chambers*, *The Lyon in Mourning* by Bishop Robert Forbes, *The Lord of the Isles* by Sir Walter Scott, *The Peat Flame Fire* by Alisdair MacGregor, *Tales of the Highlands* by James MacDonald, *The Search for Morag* by Elizabeth Campbell, *The Journal of Rev W. Mason 1895*, *Tales of the Highlands, by a Mod Medallist* by James MacDonald,

Gaelic Gatherings, or the Highlanders at Home on Heather, River and Loch by RR McIan, *Smuggling in the Highlands* by Ian MacDonald, *Moidart Among The Clanranalds* by Charles MacDonald, *A Companion and Useful Guide to the Beauties of Scotland* by Sarah Murray, *The Book of Balcardine* by Alexander Campbell Fraser, *Culloden and the Last Clansman* by James Hunter, *North Uist in History and Legend* by Bill Lawson, *Scottish Battles* by John Sadler, *The Jacobite Dictionary* by Mairead McKerracher

*The companion book to Blood Beneath Ben Nevis,
also by Mark Bridgeman*

The River Runs Red -
True Stories of Murder, Mystery and Deception
from Highland Perthshire's Dark Past.
£9.99

Aberfeldy - The History of a Highland Community
by Ruary Mackenzie Dodds. A comprehensive history
of Aberfeldy and the surrounding area with 150
black and white photos. £16.99

A Winter Journey by James Millar.
Atmospheric winter photography - 70 colour and
black and white photos. £9.99

Winter in Glen Lyon by Jamie Grant.
A hardback collection of 109 stunning
black and white photographs. Was £25, now £15.

A Doctor in the Wilderness by Walter Yellowlees.
Thirty-three years as a GP, organic gardener, writer
and lecturer, viewed through the author's experience
living and working in the Aberfeldy area. £12.99

*For more reading about the history of Fort William
and the Lochaber area, visit The Highland Bookshop*

OTHER TITLES FROM TIPPERMUIR BOOKS

Spanish Thermopylae (2009)

Battleground Perthshire (2009)

Perth: Street by Street (2012)

Born in Perthshire (2012)

In Spain with Orwell (2013)

Trust (2014)

Perth: As Others Saw Us (2014)

Love All (2015)

A Chocolate Soldier (2016)

The Early Photographers of Perthshire (2016)

Taking Detective Novels Seriously: The Collected Crime Reviews of Dorothy L Sayers (2017)

Walking with Ghosts (2017)

No Fair City: Dark Tales from Perth's Past (2017)

The Tale o the Wee Mowdie that wantit tae ken wha keeched on his heid (2017)

Hunters: Wee Stories from the Crescent: A Reminiscence of Perth's Hunter Crescent (2017)

A Little Book of Carol's (2018)

Flipstones (2018)

Perth: Scott's Fair City: The Fair Maid of Perth & Sir Walter Scott – A Celebration & Guided Tour (2018)

God, Hitler, and Lord Peter Wimsey: Selected Essays, Speeches and Articles by Dorothy L Sayers (2019)

Perth & Kinross: A Pocket Miscellany: A Companion for Visitors and Residents (2019)

The Piper of Tobruk: Pipe Major Robert Roy, MBE, DCM (2019)

The 'Gig Docter o Athole': Dr William Irvine & The Irvine Memorial Hospital (2019)

Afore the Highlands: The Jacobites in Perth, 1715–16 (2019)

'Where Sky and Summit Meet': Flight Over Perthshire – A History: Tales of Pilots, Airfields, Aeronautical Feats, & War (2019)

Diverted Traffic (2020)

Authentic Democracy: An Ethical Justification of Anarchism (2020)

'If Rivers Could Sing': A Scottish River Wildlife Journey. A Year in the Life of the River Devon as it flows through the Counties
of Perthshire, Kinross-shire & Clackmannanshire (2020)

A Squatter o Bairnrhymes (2020)

In a Sma Room Songbook: From the Poems by William Soutar (2020)

The Nicht Afore Christmas: the much-loved yuletide tale in Scots (2020)

Ice Cold Blood (2021)

The Perth Riverside Nursery & Beyond: A Spirit of Enterprise and Improvement (2021)

Fatal Duty: The Scottish Police Force to 1952: Cop Killers, Killer Cops & More (2021)

The Shanter Legacy: The Search for the Grey Mare's Tail (2021)

'Dying to Live': The Story of Grant McIntyre, Covid's Sickest Patient (2021)

The Black Watch and the Great War (2021)

Beyond the Swelkie: A Collection of Poems & Writings to Mark the Centenary of George Mackay Brown (2021)

Sweet F.A. (2022)

A War of Two Halves (2022)

A Scottish Wildlife Odyssey (2022)

In the Shadow of Piper Alpha (2022)

Mind the Links: Golf Memories (2022)

Perthshire 101: A Poetic Gazetteer of the Big County (2022)

The Banes o the Turas: An Owersettin in Scots o the Poems bi Pino Mereu scrievit in Tribute tae Hamish Henderson (2022)

Walking the Antonine Wall: A Journey from East to West Scotland (2022)

The Japan Lights: On the Trail of the Scot Who Lit Up Japan's Coast (2023)

Fat Girl Best Friend: 'Claiming Our Space' – Plus Size Women in Film & Television (2023)

Wild Quest Britain: A Nature Journey of Discovery through England, Scotland & Wales – from Lizard Point to Dunnet Head (2023)

Guid Mornin! Guid Nicht! (2023)

Madainn Mhath! Oidhche Mhath! (2023)

Who's Aldo? (2023)

A History of Irish Republicanism in Dundee (c1840 to 1985) (Rùt Nic Foirbeis, 2024)

The Stone of Destiny & The Scots (John Hulbert, 2024)

FORTHCOMING

William Soutar: Complete Poetry, Volumes I & II (Published Work) (Paul S Philippou (Editor-in-Chief) & Kirsteen McCue and Philippa Osmond-Williams (editors), 2024)

William Soutar: Complete Poetry, Volume III (Miscellaneous & Unpublished Poetry) (Paul S Philippou (Editor-in-Chief) & Kirsteen McCue and Philippa Osmond-Williams (editors), 2025)

William Soutar: Complete Poetry, Volume IV (Prose Selections) (Paul S Philippou (Editor-in-Chief) & Kirsteen McCue and Philippa Osmond-Williams (editors), 2026)

The Whole Damn Town (Hannah Ballantyne, 2024)

Balkan Rhapsody (Maria Kassimova-Moisset, translated by Iliyana Nedkova Byrne, 2024)

The Black Watch From the Crimean War to the Second Boer War (Derek Patrick and Fraser Brown, 2024)

Salvage (Mark Baillie, 2024).

All Tippermuir Books titles are available from bookshops and online booksellers. They can also be purchased directly (with free postage & packing (UK only) – minimum charges for overseas delivery) from
www.tippermuirbooks.co.uk